DELIVERING THE RIGHT STUFF

How the Airlines' Evolution in Human Factors Delivered Safety and Operational Excellence

ANDREW J. DINGEE

ISBN: 978-1-4834-8712-0 (sc)
ISBN: 978-1-4834-8713-7 (hc)
ISBN: 978-1-4834-8711-3 (e)

Library of Congress Control Number: 2018907215

Lulu Publishing Services rev. date: 07/12/2018

Learning about human factors across domains is one of the most important contributions that safety professionals can make to their own industry. From someone at the heart of one of those industries comes this new book. Eminently readable, enriched by experiences and stories, Dingee takes the reader through the use and limits of procedures, collaboration, communication, standardization, just culture, prospective memory, organizational learning and more. It will inspire you to identify and put in place the conditions for the professionals in your organization to deliver the right stuff.

Sidney Dekker, PhD
Professor
Director, Safety Science Innovation Lab, Griffith University

For anyone one who wants to better understand the journey over time in the quest for zero commercial airline accidents, this book is a must read. Andrew Dingee explains in a clear and well laid out story, the hard learned lessons that have contributed to the current high levels of safety and performance. Many of the practices and principles illustrated have natural applications in other complex settings including healthcare.

William R. Berry, MD, MPH, MPA. FACS
Associate Director – Ariadne Labs
Principal Research Scientist
Department of Health Policy and Management
Harvard T.H. Chan School of Public Health
Chief Implementation Officer
Interim Director Implementation Platform – Ariadne Labs

This book is chocked loaded in useful frontline tools. Tools which will move the needle both operationally and in safety. If you want to make a difference to your operating system by reducing human error – this is a must read.

Paul Shupe, MD, IronMan Sports Medicine Institute, UT Orthopedics, Houston TX.

For Valerie

Acknowledgements

There's been an incalculable amount of people that are responsible for shaping and supporting the creation of this book. I would like to thank my grandfather, a former P-51 fighter pilot, who awakened the love of flying within me.

Professionally, I am forever in debt to Lora Mullins, John McCoy, Michael Fant, Captain JR Russell, Jack Rubino M.D., Captain Marc Champion, the Air Line Pilot Association, the line pilot and Mary Morahan. Without your support, this book would only be a thought.

Freedom does not come without a price. This book is dedicated to all the men and women who have given the ultimate sacrifice for our great nation. Marines like Capt. Mark Gruber — my best friend.

Most of all, I would like to thank Valerie, the love of my life. Our children: Paiger, Kaitlin, Mark, Kelsey, and Grant. My parents, Jay, Doris, and Mary Lee. I would also like to thank a group of individuals — flight instructors. Because of them, I am able to write this book. But all the glory goes to God.

Contents

"Human rather than technical failures now represent the greatest threat to complex and potentially hazardous systems."
Dr. James Reason

The "Swiss Cheese" model of accident causation is a model used in risk management, nuclear engineering, and in commercial aviation. It is the safety principle behind what is known as "defense in depth."

Dr. James Reason developed the "Swiss Cheese" model in which he compares a corporate safety system to multiple slices of Swiss cheese, stacked side by side such that the risk of a threat becoming an accident is mitigated by the differing types of defenses that are layered behind each slice of cheese. When your operating system has a hole in every piece of cheese (hence Swiss cheese), then your organization is exposed to a Tier 1 accident – a fatality.

In the 1970s, the airlines suffered several major fatal aircraft accidents – holes in each layer of their safety system.

Investigations into each of these major accidents pushed beyond labeling them human error and focused on understanding the human's role in the accident. This drive to understand why pilots make mistakes led the investigators to what is now called **Human Factors.** With a deeper understanding of how humans (pilots) played a role in these accidents, the industry was able to fill in the holes of the Swiss cheese analogy and deliver zero accidents over the last two decades.

Today, when you board a U.S. legacy airline, you can be assured you have joined an organization that is committed to be the highest reliable organization on the planet. Human Factors has delivered the following statistics.

In 2017, the U.S. airline industry flew over 849.3 million people on 9.7 million flights. All of them landed without a

Human factors entails a multidisciplinary effort to generate and compile information about human capabilities and limitations and apply that information to equipment / facilities, procedures and interpersonal worker relationships for safe, effective human performance.

xiii

single fatality. In fact, you would have to go back to November 2001 to find the last crew-caused fatal accident in the United States among legacy carriers. That's 154 *million* flights ago! When you board a commercial airplane in the United States you are safer than any other place in your entire life. The odds of being involved in a fatal accident are greater for:

- Medical error – 250,000 (John Hopkins 2016);
- Motor vehicle accident – 32,166 (U.S. Department of Transportation – DOT 2016);
- Train accident – 760 (Federal Railroad Administration 2017);
- Falling from heights – 364 (U. S. Occupational Safety and Health Administration – OSHA 2016);
- Being struck by an object – 90 (OSHA 2016);
- Being electrocuted – 81 (OSHA 2016);
- Being caught between objects – 67 (OSHA 2016);
- Being struck by lightning – 38 (NOAA 2016); or
- Being killed by a dog – 31 (dogbites.org).

That's right! You have a thirty-one times greater risk of being attacked and killed by a dog than being in an accident on a U.S. legacy air carrier. Incredibly, the airlines' success has come at a time when the industry has more than doubled in size. How did they do it? Corporate leadership's drive to understand human factors evolved the airlines into what is known as a High Reliable Organization.

There is no argument that the industry that carries hundreds of millions of people per year in aluminum tubes needs to be high reliable. But it requires a blend of leadership support and specifically designed tools used by frontline employees to achieve consistent operational results, not just lectures on human factors. Walk into any airline's corporate office or look into the cockpit of any aircraft and you will quickly see the necessary traits of a HRO in action. They are:

- Standardized Operating Procedures (foundation for a lean program);

- Corporate preoccupation with failure (not the preoccupation of the frontline!);
- Focus on simplification;
- Training programs focused on work procedures;
- Commitment to organizational learning; and
- Desire to learn about human error in the operational context.

The last trait, a desire to learn about human error in the operational context, can only be fully applied after all of the preceding traits have been accomplished. Otherwise, lectures on human factors will not have the intended impact on your safety system. This last characteristic is key to understanding each chapter in my book. Understanding how humans err will help your organization when you redesign your safety system to prevent or trap human error. And one individual that knows it better than anyone is Dr. Daniel Kahneman.

> Human performance is really a result of just how situationally aware (SA) you are. SA is the result of the brain processing numerous bits of information arriving at some idea of the surrounding environment.

Daniel Kahneman received the Nobel Prize in Economics for his recent book, *Thinking Fast and Slow (2016)*, which explains how humans make decisions. Kahneman defined our brain as two computer processors. One processor delivers speed and the other delivers reliability. With this understanding, Kahneman highlighted our processors' strengths and weaknesses and delivered the key to understanding why our workers make mistakes.

The first processor delivers speed and is called System 1. It is our subconscious. It's automatic. It is fast (it handles up to 100,000 bits of information per second). It is instinctive and emotional. System 1 uses first impressions and patterns to make quick decisions based on incomplete information – not always good decision in high-risk operations. In order to work this way, System 1 has been designed to be a parallel processor. It can multi-task and is responsible for building our **situational awareness.**

System 1 doesn't require concentration or conscious thought. Instead, it works idling in the background during routine activities. A simple example of our System 1 working is our daily drive to work – a complex activity that we do effortlessly and with low energy. We don't think of each step when we drive a car down a busy interstate. System 1 delivers speed when doing routine work.

> Situational awareness is the perception of the environmental elements and events with respect to time or space, the comprehension of their meaning, and the projection of their status after some variable has changed, such as time (Endsley 1988)

When System 1 runs into difficulty, our brains activate System 2 to help. System 2 is our conscious processor. It requires us to use our full attention while executing a given task. System 2 is a serial processor that can only handle one piece of information at a time (it handles up to 15 bits of information per second). Therefore, it is a slow processor. We use System 2 to answer open-ended questions, make a career change, or anytime we need to collect information to make an important, thoughtful decision. One interesting experiment, performed by Alter et al. (2007) found that simply changing the legibility of the font used in a common cognitive test made people more likely to engage System 2. This is why you will see boxes or **bold font** in this book. I need you to engage System 2 in order to retain important information within each chapter.

As soon as your decision is made or you're done reading the **bold font**, you will turn off System 2 and System 1 takes over. We need System 1 to be fast because the alternative of activating System 2 continuously is an impossibility. System 2 is too slow for us to be efficient.

Perhaps you have heard the term **chronic unease** where corporate leaders request that frontline workers continue to activate System 2 (looking for risk) in order to prevent human error. No doubt performing routine work with System 2 activated could reduce human error but

> Chronic unease is a state of psychological strain in which an individual experiences discomfort and concern about the control of risks. (Fruhen, et al. 2013).

it is an impossible request. To constantly question your own thinking ("what if...") would be tedious and inefficient, hence unrealistic. The corporate slogan advocating for chronic unease needs to remain at the corporate level where leaders develop and deliver tools to the frontline – simple tools that deliver operational excellence based on the understanding of how we make decisions while working.

Here's a simple demonstration of how our two processors work. Recite the months of the year as fast as you can from January to December. Now, recite the months of the year backward starting at December. Did you feel the cognitive strain when you operated System 2? Did you notice the time difference to accomplish the same task but utilizing your different processors? Did you make errors when reciting the months backwards?

Corporate leadership at the airlines has learned how pilots make errors in the operational context of work and discovered that there are challenges and conflicts between our two processors. System 1 may deliver speed but it has weaknesses; weaknesses that are labeled cognitive biases. These include confirmation bias (the inclination to look for or remember information in a way that supports or confirms our already existing beliefs), plan continuation bias (the unconscious bias to continue with our original plan in spite of changing situations), and expectation bias (the situation where our biases subconsciously impact our decisions) to name just a few. Kahneman (2016) states that these biases allow human error into our safety system during routine work. His claim is validated by multiple research studies that have proven the greatest error rate for humans occurs during routine work (System 1 failures):

- For airline pilots, 76.3% of all errors;
- For the oil and gas industry, 67% of all errors; and
- For maritime accidents, 58.5% of all errors (Grech and Horberry 2002).

Since System 1 is responsible for building one's situational awareness, it will be a common theme in my book. But understanding the processor responsible for building it will lead to key tools that can be introduced into your safety system. In fact, losing situational awareness is typically caused by poor team communication and lack of standardization (Sneddon, Mearns, and Flin 2006). Improving communication and creating standardization for your organization is the first step in becoming a high reliable organization.

System 2 (the conscious mode) is our reliable processor but it comes at a cost. Two of the most significant weaknesses of System 2 are channelized attention and time-sharing. Channelized attention is similar to using a straw to focus on a switch or to read a line in a procedure. By looking through a straw to conduct work, you degrade your ability to get more information regarding your environment – you lose situational awareness. You are familiar with the effects. When you read a text while driving your car you activate System 2. How high is your situational awareness of the car braking in front of you?

The second weakness of System 2 is time-sharing where you switch rapidly from task to task. System 2 will sometimes switch back to the wrong task at the wrong time. This switching can occur at a delicate moment, causing a skipped important task in a procedure or an item on a checklist. When time-sharing is required for work activities, distractions can begin the sequence of events that can cause an accident.

With a firm understanding of how our two processors work, corporate leaders can build an operating system that prevents and traps human errors.

In order to demonstrate the three-decade progression of human factors within the airline industry, my book will review major airline accidents that changed the industry. It started with accident investigators who rejected the acceptance of pilot error on accident reports and instead learned about pilot error. Furthermore, the learnings from these accidents provided the corrective actions to make the industry safer – the same corrective actions that could make your industry safer.

My book's objective isn't to make the nervous flier more nervous. It is just the opposite. You have or will board an aircraft that is part of the safest system that has ever been designed by humans. It is a safety system that

I entrust to carry my children. The purpose of reviewing these aircraft accidents is to help you understand that your accidents are not just "pilot" error either. On the contrary, the purpose is to help you redesign your safety system with lessons learned from an industry that learned how pilots make mistakes. It is about designing your safety system for a threshold change in human quality. After all, the odds are thirty-one times greater that you will die by a dog attack than taking a commercial airline flight. It's time to fasten your seat belt.

References:

Alter, Adam L.; Oppenheimer, Daniel M.; Eply, Nicholas; and Eyre, Rebecca N. 2007. "Overcoming Intuition: Metacognitive Difficulty Activates Analytic Reasoning." *Journal of Experimental Psychology: General.* 136: 4: 569-576.

Endsley, Mica R. 1988. "Design and Evaluation for Situation Awareness Enhancement." *Proceedings of the Human Factors and Ergonomics Society Annual Meeting.* 32:2:97-101.

Fruhen, L. S.; Flin, R. H.; McLeod, R. 2013. "Chronic unease for safety managers: a conceptualization." *Journal of Risk Research* 17:8.

Grech, Michelle R.; Horberry, Tim; and Smith, Andrew. 2002. "Human Error in Maritime Operations: Analysis of Accident Reports Using the Leximancer Tool." *Proceedings of the Human Factors and Ergonomics Society Annual Meeting* 46:19:1718-1721.

Kahneman, Daniel. 2011. *Thinking Fast and Slow.* New York: Farrar, Straus and Giroux.

Sneddon, Anne; Mearns, Kathryn; and Flin, Rhona. 2006. Safety and situation awareness in offshore crews. *Cognition, Technology & Work* 8:255-267; 10.1007/s10111-006-0040-1.

U.S. Department of Transportation, Federal Aviation Administration, Human Factors Policy, 9550.8, 27 October 1993.

1

Introduction

"An idea can be as flawless as can be, but its
execution will always be full of mistakes."
Lt. Gen Brent Scowcroft (Ret.)

Lt. General Brent Scowcroft's leadership transcends both generations and political boundaries. As a top national security expert with decades of experience, he has planned and had oversight of countless missions. His quote highlights that too many times he has seen execution go astray from human error. He is keenly aware that even the best humans will err during execution. Therefore, you better plan for human error during execution.

But too many times in business, our plan assumes that the human is flawless. Any corporation that wants to move the needle to the seventh sigma level of success must acknowledge that the human is flawed. And this acknowledgement starts with corporate leadership who must drive the organization to understand human error and provide tools to frontline workers that will prevent, trap, and mitigate human error. This chapter is designed to highlight frontline tools that I have used during routine work (System 1) – tools that were developed with an understanding that I am human and that I will make mistakes.

In 2007, I entered a commercial airline operation center to locate the captain of my flight. We were assigned to fly an Airbus 320 from Denver to Phoenix. I had never flown with the captain before but that is normal for the industry.

Through the years, airline companies have become dependent on standardization based on the fundamentals of step-by-step procedures designed to deliver operational excellence. Standardization is the bedrock of operational excellence. Its goal is to deliver a logical, efficient, safe, and predictable means of carrying out mission objectives based on capturing years of best practices. Standardization has proven that in the middle of a busy flight, you can pluck one pilot from the cockpit and replace that pilot with another without impacting performance of the team. It was the only way the airline industry could grow from a handful of highly skilled aviators in the early 1900s into a workforce of over 100,000 pilots in the U.S. today. You can't scale an organization or an industry without standardization.

Because I was unfamiliar with him, I decided that the gentleman who was printing off flight paperwork was probably my captain. I approached him and asked, "Are you headed to Phoenix?" He stuck his hand out and introduced himself and I returned the favor. We covered the niceties as we pulled the remaining required flight paperwork from the computer system.

Every flight is meticulously planned for efficiency and safety. Each requires a packet of flight paperwork that consists of the aircraft's maintenance history, the filed route of flight, passenger and cargo load (for weight purposes), flight attendant names, and the weather forecasts for the departure city, en route and at our destination. We were in the planning phase of our flight and it was our opportunity to adjust the plan prior to execution in order to maintain our high safety standards and an on-time schedule.

The maintenance history and status of the airplane was exceptionally clean. Our Airbus 320 had only two deferred items and neither item impacted efficiency or safety. (Deferred is the term that allows a minor maintenance item to be carried forward until an opportunity exists for the maintenance team to fix it. Typically, deferred items get fixed when the aircraft goes to the hangar with larger maintenance issues. The regulator – the U.S. Federal Aviation Administration (FAA) – tightly monitors these deferred items.)

Next, we reviewed the weather for our route to Phoenix. When a destination is on a southerly heading from Denver, it is likely that you will depart from Runway 28 (westerly). The captain and I both commented on the high winds we experienced on our drive to the airport and knew that the likelihood of severe crosswinds on the north/south runways would limit departures. Therefore, we wanted to make sure we got off the gate expeditiously in order to get into the conga line in the event the winds limited Denver to just two departure runways. For the cruise portion of the flight, the weather report did not highlight any reports of severe turbulence. On the surface, the winds were forecasted to gust up to 40 knots for the next several hours. Phoenix was clear and calm as the front had already moved through their area.

We gathered the flight paperwork and our suitcases. We walked out of operations and entered the passenger terminal. On the walk to our assigned gate, we chatted about each other's personal lives. When we reached our gate, the captain pulled the gate agent aside and delivered an efficient, standardized brief that set expectations for her and aligned the team for execution. We entered the jet bridge and approached the door of the aircraft. The captain stepped inside. I followed him into the cockpit and placed my suitcase in the designated area, glanced around for any abnormalities or maintenance stickers, and placed my coffee in its resting place – a cup holder.

Now it was time for me to step outside and conduct the preflight on our aircraft. I exited the jet bridge, stepped onto the busy, hectic ramp, and walked to the exact point where my training had taught me to start my external preflight inspection.

All pilots are vulnerable to error and entering the ramp is the first place it can happen. The ramp at any airport is fraught with interruptions and distractions that could allow you to miss a critical step or item on the preflight. I descended down the staircase. It was loud! The aircraft next door had just pushed back and was starting its engines. I reached for my earplugs and inserted them. With my loss of hearing, my situational awareness on the ramp decreased and I had to keep my head on a swivel looking for threats.

I wrapped up my preflight and headed over to the stairs that led to the jet bridge. As always, I looked over the aircraft one last time as an integrity check and to build situational awareness on what and who was around the aircraft. After all, our Airbus didn't have side view mirrors to see who was behind us. These would have been helpful during our pushback. I entered the jet bridge, slid by the boarding passengers, and entered the cockpit. The Captain asked, "How does she look?" I replied, "No issues." I settled into the right seat of the aircraft and began setting up the cockpit switches and systems that were within my areas of responsibility.

I cannot overstate the disruptiveness of distractions when following procedures. Setting up a cockpit is a fluid, ever-changing process. Crews must be able to balance safety and efficiency all under the pressure of being on time. A technique taught to combat distractions is – if interrupted by a gate agent, a flight attendant, or the captain – to leave your hand on the switch. This technique incorporates multiple sensory inputs and a higher level of task attentiveness is achieved. It also activates System 2, which has a very low error rate. Furthermore, this allows you to remember where you left off and what the next task will be. It eliminates the possibility of accidently skipping a step and suffering the consequences.

I utilized my aircraft flows (we will discuss more about what flows are in Chapter 5) and finished testing the multiple systems on board that needed to be working prior to our pushback. I updated the Phoenix weather and took a breath. All my pre-departure responsibilities were complete.

This natural pause in our work allowed the captain to initiate the pre-departure brief. The purpose of this brief is to adjust the plan in the event we find changes such as changes to aircraft status, weather, the airport, or the crew. Briefs are what connect the plan to the execution. They are standardized in order to be efficient and they align the team prior to beginning work.

Since 50% of airline accidents have miscommunication between crews as a contributing cause (Flight Safety Foundation 1990), the airlines have spent considerable time teaching and developing standard briefings. Furthermore, the quality of the brief directly influences the performance of the team during execution. Today, my captain delivered a detailed, chronological brief that aligned our mental models of our upcoming work – details that covered the taxi plan, takeoff procedures, and the initial climb. Another brief would cover the approach and landing, but that would be done prior to descent. Details are important in every brief. Runway incursions are one of the top threats in the industry and his detailed brief allowed us to be aligned for the busy taxi out. He also highlighted hazards and discussed how to mitigate those hazards along the taxi plan. Standard briefs deliver operational excellence.

With the expected workflow covered, the captain moved on to the next section of the brief – emergencies. He reviewed what we would do if we encountered an engine failure on takeoff – a critical procedure but rare occurrence. While he reviewed the emergency procedure, he touched each switch in order to prime his muscle memory. He was finished in two minutes.

With mental models aligned, it was time for the "Before Pushback Checklist." This checklist is not a TO DO checklist. Instead, consider it a human factor checklist. It is specifically designed to trap human error. In other words, human factor checklists are designed to go back and verify that critical steps in our procedures have been completed – to catch mistakes. Their effectiveness rests on two key ingredients. The first one is methodology. Human factor checklists utilize CHALLENGE and RESPONSE. The second ingredient is what is written on the checklist. Each item is critical to review and often the cause of major accidents. Human factor checklists are designed to wake up System 2 (delivering reliability) and trap these human errors. In fact, this simple checklist is what separates the airline safety record from all other industries' safety records. We will discuss more about human factor checklists in Chapter 5.

With the "Before Pushback Checklist" complete, it was time to move to the next phase of our journey – work, or in this case, fly! The next sequence of our flight is called pushing back. It sounds like a simple procedure. The ground crew pushes our aircraft back a hundred yards. Pushbacks have been fatal, but the airline industry has been successful at delivering zero fatal accidents through the creation of standard callouts. I will review how standard callouts changed the industries accident record in Chapter 6.

For our flight, here's how standard callouts delivered operational efficiencies without sacrificing safety. The captain checked in with the lead ramper, establishing radio communication between the two. With a good radio check, the lead ramp worker stated, "Ready for pushback." This callout assured the captain that the aircraft had been inspected, that no equipment was in the way, and that all personnel were in their designated position to start the pushback. These are the conditions that must be met prior the tug driver's callout. The captain responded, "Stand by" to the tug operator.

At the captain's request, I called ramp tower and asked permission to push. We were given clearance to push and I informed the captain that ramp tower had cleared us.

The captain told the lead ramper, "Brakes released, cleared to push" and the lead ramper responded, "Roger, cleared to push" – a communication crosscheck on the status of the aircraft and clearance from another party.

Our aircraft began to move backwards and away from the gate. The lead ramper stopped the aircraft at the designated stopping point and again the captain and the lead ramper went through the "pushback" callout plan in order to ensure both their safety and ours.

Once completed, the lead ramper walked to a predetermined spot, rendered a smart, crisp salute that indicated that all pushback members and the tug were clear of the aircraft and that it was safe to taxi the aircraft away from the pushback spot. The captain returned the salute with a simple flash of the taxi light, acknowledging that the ramp was clear and that we were on our own. The pushback phase of our flight was complete and without incident because of both team's high situational awareness.

The captain asked me to start engine number one. I initiated the engine starting sequence and the large turbofan engine came to life. The generator came online at 47% and the engine reached a comfortable idle speed. All was good with the number one engine. I initiated the start sequence for the second engine. After the second engine achieved idle, I conducted my post engine procedure flows with my callout, "Clear right." The captain moved the throttles forward and our 150,000-pound aircraft began to roll. We were in the taxi phase of the operation.

The captain taxied the aircraft to a specific ramp area where ground control would give us directions to taxi to Runway 28.

As a first officer on board a commercial airliner, the taxi sequence is one of the highest workload-intensive phases of flight. I have to determine the final weight of the aircraft, set the trim, configure the aircraft for takeoff, crosscheck the captain's taxi route, handle the communications with ground control, and read the "Before Takeoff Checklist." This phase provides an opportune time to err and the airlines know that. I have and I will make mistakes during this phase. By definition, it is routine work because I rely on System 1 to conduct my workflows. We have learned the weaknesses of System 1 and this is a critical phase of flight operations. So, the airlines have lowered risk in this phase by implementing Crew Resource Management (CRM) programs. And in this environment, we are specifically trained to recognize one element of CRM called **workload** management.

Workload management is affected by multiple factors such as stress, fatigue, illness, and fitness. Poor workload management leads to poor decision-making.

If I miss radio calls, use the wrong call sign, or am late on moving switches,

> Workload refers to the **demands** imposed on a user by the task, and the **capacity** of the user to meet those demands. Workload management is a critical element of CRM.

these are indicators to the captain that I am behind on my workload and that I am susceptible to making a mistake. CRM courses teach crews how to recognize when someone is behind on their procedures. Furthermore, these courses deliver solutions on how to manage the team's progress. Captains can manage my workflow by taxiing slower, telling me not to rush or finding a place ahead of us to stop. These simple techniques allow me to catch up but also highlight how the aviation system acknowledges that the human will make a mistake.

With my taxi procedures completed, I counted the aircraft in front of us. We were number three for departure. At this time, the captain called for the "Before Takeoff Checklist." The "Before Takeoff Checklist" is built with the same principles of the "Before Pushback Checklist." This checklist contains only the critical items that are required in order to get safely airborne. When I read any human factor checklist and the response isn't the scripted response on the checklist, I stop the job and correct my error. It is the most simplistic and effective "stop the job" program that I have seen.

Tower called us and gave us clearance to line up and wait. The captain powered up both engines and utilized his left hand to move the tiller bar turning the aircraft onto the runway. We waited for takeoff clearance from tower. The wind speed was blowing from the south at over 32 knots. Denver Tower issued our takeoff clearance and the captain turned the aircraft control over to me. I pushed the throttles forward to takeoff power and the Pratt and Whitney engines roared to life. I smoothly released the brakes and we instantly accelerated down the runway. In order to keep the aircraft on centerline, I placed the yoke to the left to counter the strong southerly wind. We reached rotation speed and I rotated to a 15-degree pitch. With a positive climb rate, the captain reached over and raised the landing gear. I could hear the gear enter the wheel bays and the loud wind speed lessened as the landing gear doors closed. We were on our way to Phoenix.

The controllers turned us south toward Phoenix and we continued our climb to our final altitude. The light turbulence that is common at Denver smoothed out passing 14,000 feet and a few minutes later we arrived at our cruising altitude. The captain asked Denver Center if there were any reports of turbulence. Denver Center asked a FEDEX aircraft that was 1,000 feet above us and crossing our route, "How's the ride, FEDEX?" FEDEX answered, "Smooth." With no significant weather advisories for turbulence, no adverse reports with Denver, and FEDEX responding with smooth air, the captain turned off the seat belt sign and delivered his welcome announcement to our passengers.

Geographically, we were flying over the Great Sand Dunes National Park and Reserve in Colorado. The Park is located in the south central region of Colorado. The dunes are the largest sand dunes in North America. They rise to over 750 feet above the valley floor and continue to grow every year. Their source of sand comes from the strong winds that carry the sand from the plains or the glacier erosion created centuries ago. We looked down at the sand dunes and both commented about the amount of sand that was being blown into the air below us.

Moments later, we noticed the airspeed trend indicator. It showed that we were rapidly accelerating by an additional 50 knots. The airplane was quickly entering the red warning over-speed regime, which is an unsafe condition. I commented on the acceleration to the captain as I disengaged the autopilot and the auto-throttle systems. As the engines slowed to idle, we were still way too fast, so I initiated a small climb in order to bleed more airspeed off before the warning system activated. Suddenly, the aircraft violently and rapidly rolled to the right and the nose pitched down. If you have ever been to a rodeo, imagine being the bull rider and trying to hang on to the bull with one hand. I immediately applied full left stick and nose aft to keep our A320 upright. It didn't work and we continued the hard roll to the right. Without the seat belts on, I would have been thrown out of the chair and onto the cockpit window. The roll rate was so sudden and severe, it felt as if we would go upside down. My attention became completely **channelized** on only one instrument – the cockpit indicator that informed me which way was up.

Finally, the aircraft stopped rolling to the right as we approached the 70-degree

> Channelized Attention is when someone focuses all conscious attention on a limited number of environmental cues to the exclusion of others of a subjectively equal or higher or more immediate priority, leading to an unsafe situation. (Department of Defense Human Factors Analysis and Classification System, 2007)

mark on our attitude indicator. She was slowly responding to our input and the wings began to level to the horizon. I began to pull up on the nose and brought the throttles to idle in order to slow our descent and rapidly rising airspeed. This type of scenario is called an unusual attitude or loss of control and we had practiced it many times in airline simulators. As a former fighter pilot, I lived upside down in an aircraft, but never dreamed of going inverted in an Airbus.

Seconds later, a second severe burst of turbulence hit our aircraft. It was the same rodeo ride. The aircraft rolled rapidly to the right and the nose dropped again. Initially, it felt like our input didn't stop the rapid rolling or the low nose condition. On this second encounter, I began to formulate a way to utilize a barrel roll without using our rudder (an advance fighter maneuver) in order to protect our customers in the cabin. But like the previous encounter, I began to get control of our aircraft around 70 degrees bank angle. Our aircraft procedures for loss of control focus on **not** utilizing the rudder to control the rolling aircraft. Thanks to my training, my feet were firmly on the floor and I continued to dampen out the multiple oscillations using just the ailerons. A few seconds later we flew out of the turbulence and I leveled our Airbus thousands of feet below our initial altitude. We were still very nose low and I initiated a low nose recovery. The captain gave me control of the radios. "Ding." The chime made me look down and notice that our displays showed multiple flight computer failures. We hit one more turbulent wave (mild compared to the previous two) and exited the severe turbulence.

The captain confirmed that I had control of the aircraft and I repeated that I had control of the aircraft (another valuable procedure learned from an aircraft accident). The captain called the lead flight attendant to determine if anybody on board had been injured during the severe turbulence encounter.

Our A320 had electronic checklists (these are TO DO checklists not human factor checklists) and I started to follow them, step-by-step, in order to reset our flight computers. As I reset each flight computer, the TO DO item disappeared on these electronic checklists. An electronic checklist that receives feedback from switches is fundamental in catching errors while following the checklist. Eventually, I was able to reset all the flight digital computers and our aircraft returned to normal flight status.

I contacted Denver Center and declared an emergency. Denver Center, always the professional controllers, assigned us a heading to the airport and a safe altitude to which to descend.

The captain leaned over and told me we had injuries in the cabin. He whispered that he hoped nobody was holding on to an infant. The turbulence was so severe that no one would have been able to keep their infant in their arms. I asked Denver Center to have EMTs meet us at the gate.

During the next fifteen minutes, the captain's entire attention was channelized on talking with the flight attendants and assessing the condition of the injured passengers. What complicated this communication was the lead flight attendant was injured as well. He had just started the beverage service and the cart leapt into the air on the first encounter. As the cart descended, it landed on his lower leg, tearing a ligament. At the moment of the encounter, he was serving a freshly brewed pot of hot coffee. As the aircraft violently rolled right, he lost control of the pot of hot coffee and it landed on one of our passengers leaving second-degree burns. But the worst injury was to a woman who had gotten up to use the restroom when the turbulence hit. As the aircraft pitched nose low, it slammed her head into the ceiling. She hit with such force that her head broke through the plastic ceiling and lacerated her entire scalp. She was bleeding severely and needed immediate medical assistance.

Other than the strong winds on the surface at Denver, the weather was pleasant. I set up the flight management system for landing on Runway 16 Left. I began to slow the aircraft and configured her for landing. The captain completed the coordination of the injured passengers and realized we were within five miles of the runway and requested a quick status brief. I reviewed the aircraft status, navigational status, 16 Left approach information, weather, and requested that he crosscheck my work. He reviewed the flight management computers and the status of the aircraft. At this moment during an emergency, captains have been trained to take over and land the aircraft. However, handling the passengers in the back of the aircraft had channelized his attention and he had lower situational awareness of where we were at the time. Surprised to see how close we were from landing, the captain made the decision to have me land. His decision to not take control of the aircraft and land was an acknowledgement of the effectiveness of our airline's CRM training.

We passed over the runway lights and approached the runway. At 30 feet, I initiated the flare and pulled both engines to idle speed. At the same time, I smoothly raised the nose. I thought to myself, "I need to make this a smooth landing after what our passengers just went through." The main landing gear softly touched down. My timing in the flare was perfect. We rolled to the end of the runway and exited left onto the taxiway.

In all of my flight experiences, I had never heard this sound after a flight – applause. I could hear it through the door.

The captain taxied the aircraft to the gate where the paramedics were the first to board our aircraft. We completed our "After Parking Checklist" and opened the cockpit door. I was not ready for what I saw next. The first person we saw was the woman who went through the hard plastic ceiling of our aircraft. Her long blonde hair was completely soaked in blood and she was grimacing in pain – an instant reminder of the precious cargo that we carry. The cabin looked as if *Animal House* had been filmed in it. Suitcases, laptops, open luggage bins, and garbage were lying all over the cabin. It was a mess. One of the flight attendants came up to inform us that there were no babies on board. Both the captain and I sighed with relief.

Nowadays, complaints with the airlines consist of customer service complaints like lost luggage, poor choice of red wine, or a late arrival caused by weather. But by sharing our severe turbulence encounter, I have highlighted the airline industry defense in depth approach to high-risk activity. It is a story that demonstrates learning on the organizational level and highlights eighty years of human factor learnings based on tools that deliver a safe, reliable outcome. In the following chapters, I will review tragic accidents that helped shape these human factor tools that can transfer into your industry and deliver the same success.

References:

Department of Defense, Human Factors Analysis and Classification System (DOD HFACS) Version 7.0

Flight Safety Foundation. 1990. *Accident Prevention* 46:4 and 46:6.

2

The Evolution of Crew Resource Management

"Without CRM Training, it's a cinch we wouldn't have made it."
Captain Al Haynes

Captain Al Haynes is simply a hero. What he accomplished on July 19, 1989 was a miracle that test pilots could not replicate in flight simulators. His quote acknowledges the advantages that United Airlines CRM courses gave him on that fateful day. But CRM courses from thirty years ago are not the same today. In order to understand human factors, it is important to understand how CRM has evolved over the decades.

A few years ago, an elderly woman walked up to Gate B12 at the Minneapolis airport and asked me a simple question. "Are you flying me to Chicago?" Being a young, proud former Marine fighter pilot and newly minted Boeing 727 First Officer, I said, "Yes, Ma'am!" She quickly scanned me from head to toe and said, "You don't have enough gray hair to be my pilot." With no opportunity to explain my qualifications, she quickly turned away and walked over to the gate agent at the podium. I overheard her tell the gate agent that she would prefer to be on the next flight to Chicago. I was shocked. I thought I knew how to win her back, so I ran down the jet bridge and asked the captain to join me at the gate. He was a good sport and we walked over to the woman who was at the gate agent's podium. I proudly displayed the captain's full head of gray hair.

Still, no luck. She changed her itinerary and rebooked on the later flight to Chicago. Defeated, we safely flew to Chicago without her in seat 14C.

The elderly woman's assessment that gray hair equates to safety or experience is flawed. Yes, gray hair can be a tool to gage experience, but it doesn't guarantee an error-free flight. All of us are familiar with an accident within our organization that surprised us because a senior employee was "one of our best." In fact, "the best-of-the-best" are accountable for some of the world's worst accidents, regardless of the industry (Tenerife air crash, the sinking of the Titanic, the Josie King medical error case at Johns Hopkins Children's Center). A corporation that bases the success of its safety system solely on the seniority of its employees is deceiving itself.

Instead of hair color, leadership must strategically focus on understanding human error to improve frontline employees' decision-making. If they do not, sooner rather than later, the boardroom will be dealing with an investigation and answering questions like "how would our most experienced/best employee do that and how do we prevent it from happening again?"

If it had been December 28, 1978 and our elderly passenger met the flight crew of United Airlines Flight 173 from Denver, Colorado to Portland Oregon, she would have boarded a flight on which she "felt safe" based on the quantity of gray hair of her three pilots. She also would have boarded a flight that changed the airline industry forever. The captain of Flight 173 had over 27,600 hours of flight time and his gray hair equated to over three decades of experience in the aviation industry. His name was Captain Malburn McBroom.

Along with Captain McBroom was First Officer Beebe who had over 5,200 hours of flight time and a flight engineer who had over 3,900 hours. The experience of these three pilots equated to over fifty years, but their collective flying experience would fail them on this flight.

First Officer Beebe was the flying pilot to Portland and lifted the large Boeing 707 off the runway and turned slowly towards Portland. After two uneventful hours of flight, he began the descent toward the assigned runway. Within twenty miles of the airport, the first officer asked Captain McBroom to lower the landing gear. The captain reached for the landing gear handle and placed it into the down position.

As the landing gear began to lower, Captain McBroom and the first officer heard an abnormal vibration and felt an aggressive yaw of the aircraft. The flight crew assumed something had malfunctioned in the main landing gear as it was being lowered, but none of the indicator lights suggested a malfunction. Based on the unusual noises, the first officer leveled the aircraft off at 5,000 feet and informed Portland Approach Control that they would need vectors in order to troubleshoot what was believed to be, a malfunction with one of the main landing gears. The crew exited the Portland traffic pattern with a little over 14,000 pounds of fuel onboard – a little more than an hour of flight time.

The captain directed the flight engineer to enter the passenger cabin and visually verify that the landing gear was down by verifying that small pins were extended on the upper surface of the wings. The flight engineer returned with confirmation that the pins were visible and reread a checklist for confirmation. Twenty minutes had elapsed along with 4,000 pounds of fuel.

The captain contacted airline maintenance on a separate radio channel to discuss more procedures to validate the status of the landing gear. Even with the pin indicators confirming that the main landing gear was down and locked, the captain continued to work the scenario in the event of a main landing gear collapse on the runway while landing.

Next, the captain asked the lead flight attendant to adjust the passenger seating arrangement in the cabin. An airline employee was moved to an emergency exit window to ensure its safe operation. Within the cockpit, the crew discussed techniques on how to land the aircraft and how to hold the assumed bad landing gear off the runway as long as possible. Another twenty minutes had elapsed and the aircraft was still twenty miles from Portland Airport with less than 6,000 pounds of fuel (25 minutes).

It is important for the reader to understand that the workload in this environment is high for the entire crew. The cockpit crew is making many decisions in an environment full of distractions. They are talking with Air Traffic Controllers (ATC) regarding safe handling of the flight and with the flight attendants to ensure the safety of the passengers. They are discussing with maintenance ways to verify that the landing gear is down. They are informing the flight dispatchers about the perceived landing gear issue and calling Portland station operations to keep them updated on the status of their flight.

During all of these activities the first officer was flying a large multi-engine aircraft. Most importantly, the pilots were talking between each other, but in the hectic environment it was difficult to manage complete conversations. The crew was **task-saturated** and as they worked through these issues, one hour had quickly ticked off the clock. One hour!

> Task Saturation is having too much to do in too little time. It has been consistently identified as a contributing cause in aviation mishaps.

In the next few critical minutes, the captain briefed the cockpit crewmembers to land with 4,000 pounds of fuel on board. When this conversation occurred, the aircraft was already below 4,000 pounds of fuel and still twenty miles from the runway with the gear down. The flight engineer did some quick mental math check to determine whether landing with 4,000 pounds was achievable or not. He responded, "That's really going to run us low on fuel." Perhaps this was the flight engineer's attempt to inform the captain that there was not enough fuel onboard and that the captain's goal of landing with 4,000 pounds of fuel was not feasible. But the investigators would never be able to determine the reasoning behind the flight engineer's comments. He did not survive the impending crash.

Five more precious minutes (and 1,000 pounds of fuel) went by and the first officer, who could not see the fuel gauges, asked, "How much fuel do we have now?" The flight engineer responded, "3,000 pounds" (fifteen minutes). Perhaps the first officer had picked up on the fuel concern of the flight engineer, triggering him to ask the fuel question again. Was this an attempt to ensure that the captain heard that the fuel quantity was below the briefed landing fuel by 1,000 pounds? The repeating of 3,000 pounds of fuel by the first officer was an opportunity for the crew to recognize the significance of the low fuel on board and make it the top priority. But before the first officer or flight engineer could assert their perceived uneasiness with the fuel status, the captain again sent the flight engineer to the cabin in order to see if the cabin was ready for a possible evacuation. And the aircraft continued to burn fuel.

Amazingly, another ten minutes elapsed and 2,000 pounds of fuel burned as multiple conversations occurred. The conversations included the status of the aircraft's main landing gear, commands from ATC, and the expected arrival time with station operations. There was no conversation recorded between the captain and the first officer regarding the status of the fuel remaining onboard. With just six minutes of fuel left (less than 1,000 pounds), the lead flight attendant entered the cockpit and conversed with the captain. Their discussion covered the completion of repositioning of crewmembers within the cabin and passenger debriefs on how to open the exit windows. As the flight attendant left the cockpit, the first officer announced, "I think you just lost the number four engine."

Over the next three minutes and two seconds, the captain and the flight engineer unsuccessfully worked on rerouting the little remaining fuel to the failed engine. The first officer was flying the aircraft but initially waited to be told to head toward Portland. Thirty seconds later, he would turn the aircraft toward the runway which was twenty miles away and hopelessly out of range.

With the aircraft pointed in the right direction, incredulously the captain discussed the status of the cabin, commented on the anti-skid system, and pulled a circuit breaker. There was no discussion on the fuel status or feeling of uneasiness. This was a clear indication that the captain was still focused on the possibility that the main landing gear could collapse upon landing and not the immediate threat facing the crew – impending fuel starvation.

The aircraft was still over twelve miles away from the airport and at 5,000 feet. The landing gear was down and the flaps were in a landing configuration. The captain looked back toward the flight engineer and continued to monitor the work of the flight engineer as he attempted to feed fuel into the failed engine, but it would be too late. Seconds later, the captain said, "they're all failing."

The first officer's last transmission to Portland Tower was "Mayday our engines are flaming out. We're going down. We're not going to be able to make the airport." The Portland Tower controller was too stunned to respond. Moments later, the aircraft crashed into a wooded section of a populated area of suburban Portland about six nautical miles southeast of the airport. There was no fire at the accident site, mainly because there was no fuel left onboard the aircraft.

Eight persons died and twenty-one passengers received serious injuries. The captain and first officer survived the accident.

With black box in hand, the investigators dug into why this accident happened. How did a thump and a yaw during gear extension cause an aircraft to run out of fuel?

The investigation team focused on the dynamics of the cockpit and how the crew handled the initial landing gear malfunction. Listening to the black box, the team noticed how the stature of Captain McBroom and his management style exerted subtle pressure on his crew to conform to his way of thinking. In fact, the National Transportation Safety Board (NTSB) investigators believed that the captain's behavior influenced the interaction and adequate monitoring of the aircraft and forced the crewmembers to yield their right to express an opinion. This was demonstrated to the investigators when the flight engineer said, "Fifteen minutes is gonna run us low on fuel." The message was just "too soft" to raise a concern. His words lacked **assertiveness.**

> Assertiveness is the willingness to actively participate and the ability to state and maintain your position. (*Naval Aviation Safety School*)

Worse yet, the captain asked the flight engineer to step out of the cockpit just before the final moments before the aircraft ran out of fuel. The engineer complied rather than raising the urgency of the impending fuel crisis.

The NTSB's report determined that the cause of the accident to be:

- The failure of the captain to properly monitor the aircraft's fuel state;
- The failure of the captain to properly respond to the low fuel state; and
- The failure of the junior crewmembers' assertiveness regarding fuel state.

Combined, the above listed causes resulted in fuel exhaustion to all four engines. The NTSB highlighted that the captain's inattention resulted from preoccupation with a "supposed" landing gear malfunction and preparations for a possible emergency landing.

The NTSB also determined that the failure of the other two flight crewmembers to either fully comprehend the criticality of the fuel state or to successfully communicate their concern to the captain, was a contributing factor.

In their report, the NTSB indicated that this accident exemplified a recurring problem in the airline industry – a breakdown in teamwork during a situation involving malfunctions of aircraft systems in flight. The corrective action from this tragic accident was the creation of **Cockpit Resource Management (CRM)**.

CRM is a system of error management that is based on the goal of improving safety through acknowledgement of the human contributions to error and the implementation of effective strategies for resource utilization. (Helmreich, Merritt and Wilhelm 1999)

To move the concept of CRM forward in the airline industry, the NTSB issued an operations bulletin to all carrier operations inspectors (those who work for the Federal Aviation Administration but are assigned directly to each airline). The bulletin directed the inspectors to ensure that their flight crews were indoctrinated in the following Cockpit Resource Management principles:

- Situational Awareness;
- Decision-making;
- Communication;
- Assertiveness; and
- Leadership.

The NTSB further recommended active participation of cockpit crewmembers during training in these principles in order to assure learning versus just listening to lectures.

When you read about this accident you may have thought it was unique; that this accident could never happen again; that Flight 173 was caused by a bad pilot; or that this accident was a "one-off" and the industry had a knee-jerk reaction to it. On the contrary, this accident was merely the last one in a chain of accidents that left people wondering how qualified, highly trained teams could make such mistakes or how a person of responsibility could be preoccupied by a lower tier threat. Within Flight 173's investigation summary, the NTSB referenced a string of accidents in the industry that led to this one. All of them shared a common theme: teamwork broke down.

- On January 13, 1969 (eight years prior to Flight 173), Scandinavian Airlines System Flight 933 crashed into the ocean during an approach to Los Angeles International Airport. The green light for the nose gear failed to illuminate after the landing gear was lowered. The SAS cockpit crew became so occupied with attempting to diagnose the lack of a nose gear green light that they allowed their rate of descent to increase, until their DC-8 crashed into the Pacific Ocean.
- On December 29, 1972 (five years prior to Flight 173) Eastern Air Lines Flight 401 crashed while circling Miami International Airport. The NTSB determined that the Eastern Air Line crew became preoccupied with a nose gear indicator light problem and

accidentally disconnected the autopilot, causing the aircraft to make a slow descent and crash into the Everglades. Further investigation revealed that the nose gear was down and locked and the autopilot system did not have an alarm when it was disconnected. (More information about this accident in Chapter 6.)

- On March 27, 1977 (one year prior to Flight 173) the crew of KLM Boeing 747 initiated their takeoff roll at the Tenerife Airport and collided with another Boeing 747 from Pan Am Airlines. It is the largest fatal accident in the commercial airline industry killing 582 crewmembers and passengers. This accident became well known for the first officer's tense voice during the takeoff roll – he knew they were not cleared for takeoff because the other 747 was still on the runway. Yet he felt intimidated and unable to speak up to one of the most famous and respected captains at KLM – Captain Jacob Van Zanten.

- The December 28, 1978 United Flight 173 crash was the fifth in this series of accidents and emphasized the impact of interpersonal relationships can have on a team.

It was time for the industry to stop blaming pilots for mistakes; to evolve to an industry that understands that experienced, trained humans make errors; and to learn the reasons why people err. The industry needed to change the leadership approach – a captain's "god-like behavior" was no longer an acceptable way to lead a team.

1981 – 1st Generation CRM

After the crash of Flight 173, United Airlines initiated the industry's first CRM course in 1981. The training was developed with the aid of consultants who had developed training programs for corporations trying to enhance managerial effectiveness. The United program was modeled from a program called the 'Managerial Grid' developed by psychologists Robert Blake and Jane Mouton (Blake & Mouton, 1964). The training was conducted in a classroom setting and included participants' diagnoses of their own managerial style. These initial CRM programs emphasized differing individual styles. They included ways to correct deficiencies in individual behavior such as a lack of assertiveness by juniors and authoritarian behavior by captains. Supporting this emphasis, the NTSB singled out Flight 173's captain for failure to accept input from junior crewmembers and a lack of assertiveness by the flight engineer. First generation courses were psychological in nature with a heavy focus on psychological testing and leadership concepts. They advocated general strategies of interpersonal behavior and interaction with other team members. To deliver the concept, the CRM course employed games and exercises unrelated to aviation to illustrate the learnings. It was also recognized that CRM training should not be a single experience in a pilot's career. Rather, it should be part of annual refresher training.

Today, many corporations and hospitals utilize 1st generation CRM programs in which psychological exams are used to identify an individual's managerial style. Once armed with the results, individuals are assigned a personality type. One example of this testing is the Hartman Personality Profile (HPP) that defines personality types using the following color coded system:

- Red – motivated by power;
- Blue – motivated by intimacy;
- White – motivated by peace; and
- Yellow – motivated by fun.

Here's how HPP works. Once individuals have taken the test and the results define them as a red, for instance, they are taught how individuals assigned the colors blue, white and yellow will respond to their managerial or personality style. In the end, a team can have different personalities yet be armed with the capability to assert their concerns to any color type of leader. With this training, the team improved communication amongst team members and improved the team's decision-making.

A drawback to the HPP test is the inability of individuals to know their coworkers personality color while at work. Many corporations have solved this concern by issuing colored nametags or by providing wristbands that identify their assigned colors. But a colored wristband does not change behaviors in the workplace. There were other faults with first generation of CRM. These courses were often referred to as "charm school" and were mocked by individuals as an attempt to make them get along by being "nice." A misrepresentation for sure, but the airline industry began to see a decrease in accidents caused by the breakdown of teamwork. They also started recording more success stories that highlighted an improvement in teamwork. Then, the "impossible" happened.

1989 – 2nd Generation CRM

As 1st generation CRM was morphing into a new and improved methodology to improve teamwork, the industry received its first clear validation of the effectiveness of CRM training. In 1989, just eight years after the first CRM course at United Airlines, Captain Al Haynes would apply all that he learned and then some to solve the "impossible." Captain Haynes, a former U.S. Marine, was piloting United Airlines Flight 232, a DC-10, from Denver to Chicago. Suddenly, while at 37,000 feet, the tail-mounted number two-engine exploded, severing all three hydraulic lines that controlled the steering of the aircraft. Captain Al Haynes and his team no longer had the ability to use the yoke (steering wheel). The aircraft was traveling at 500 miles per hour with no one at the controls! The aircraft's condition was equivalent to driving 200 mph down the interstate with a steering wheel that doesn't work, a gas pedal that is stuck to the floor, and the pressure of 296 men, women, and children relying on you to have the "right stuff."

Captain Al Haynes was able to gain a very limited amount of control of the aircraft, but not through the use of the control wheel. Instead, he figured out that he could keep the aircraft "shiny side up" by adjusting the thrust levers and splitting the throttles to achieve climbs or descents. He also had limited amount of rudder to aid in turning the severely damaged aircraft. The first officer's workload was completely consumed by maintaining a double-handed bicep curl on the yoke in order to keep the aircraft from diving toward the earth. In the heat of this epic battle to get control of his aircraft, Captain Haynes coolly and calmly requested the help of a deadheading pilot (a fully qualified pilot who was riding to work and sitting in the passenger cabin), First Officer Denny Fitch.

This simple and now obvious act of utilizing any and all resources available to maintain control and aid in decision-making was taught in United's CRM courses. In fact, if you listen to the ATC tapes from the accident, you will hear how Captain Haynes' sense of humor calmed the situation and aided the team with problem solving. After all, the crew was piloting an aircraft that wasn't airworthy.

Perhaps you have seen the video of Captain Haynes and his team landing his crippled DC 10 at Sioux City, IA. If you haven't, do. It will impact you. One hundred and eleven people died on that crashed landing, but Captain Haynes and his leadership saved the lives of 186 men, women, and children because of CRM.

In 2005, I had the honor to work with Captain Haynes. The most humble of heroes, he shared with me his personal lesson learned on what he would do differently. He wouldn't select idle once over the runway. Instead, he would simply perform a power on landing. His open sharing of lessons learned would save the crew of an Airbus 300 at Baghdad after being targeted by a surface-to-air missile. Incredulously, the two airbus pilots had just seen Captain Haynes talk about his accident and they adopted his lesson learned to their flight. They calmly delivered their DHL airplane onto the runway without pirouetting into a field. Captain Haynes leadership continues to impact the aviation industry three decades later.

For UAL 232, the NTSB investigators discovered that the Number 2 engine blade failed and subsequently blew up because of a granular flaw in a single turbine blade – a granular flaw that existed during a time when maintenance equipment and procedures were unable to detect a flaw of this size in the engine blade.

After the Sioux City accident, a tradition began at United Airlines that honored Captain Hayne's leadership on that tragic day. While boarding, deadheading pilots will introduce themselves to the cockpit and flight attendant crews. This simple act is the passing on of Captain Hayne's lesson learned and a nod to the heroism on that day – a lesson that allows flight deck crews to fully utilize **all** resources available (not just those in the cockpit) in the event of an emergency.

As a result of this accident, the CRM curriculum evolved into 2nd generation. The airlines included a new course that had the participants demonstrate briefing strategies and a class on stress management. The course delivery shifted from psychology and non-aviation specific exercises to aviation-specific examples that related to flight operations. A new communication tool was taught that delivered assertiveness within a conversation to a higher-ranking worker. This tool was based on CUS words (an acronym, not a reference to a sailor's language). It allows for a junior person within the team to escalate their perspective of a situation. Here's how CUS words are utilized in the cockpit:

- I am **C**oncerned about the fuel quantity (Level 1).
- I am **U**ncomfortable about fuel quantity (Level 2).
- I believe the **S**afety of our flight is at risk with the fuel quantity levels (Level 3).

In order to escalate a situation in which a junior member recognizes the condition or status of a system, the junior crewmember begins by using the word "Concern." As it progresses, or more assertiveness is required because the first message didn't escalate the concern, the "Uncomfortable" word is used. Finally, when the attention of the senior member is needed, the "Safety" word is utilized. Hospitals are now teaching this method when nurses need doctors to listen more effectively and "really" hear their concerns.

Team members were also introduced to the understanding of James Reason's Swiss Cheese Model of accident causation (Reason 1990). With a focus on organizational causes to accidents, it taught the workforce that all workers make mistakes. The benefit of determining corporate causes from accidents allowed for more effective corrective actions as well. Just firing the worker after a mistake allows for the next worker to commit the same error. Corporate leadership began to understand that accidents were no longer "pilot error" and the shift away from the blaming culture began.

Finally, the course name changed as well. It was no longer called Cockpit Resource Management. The new course became **Crew** Resource Management and highlighted the dynamic problem-solving creativity of Captain Al Haynes on United Flight 232.

1991 – 3rd Generation CRM

Today, airline pilots are heralded as the most procedurally compliant group of all professionals. However, it wasn't always that way. To evolve into 3rd generation CRM, instead of focusing on a single accident, a study of ninety-three fatal commercial airline accidents was undertaken. Lautman and Gallimore (1990) studied these fatal aviation accidents and discovered that the leading crew-caused factor was pilot deviation from basic operational procedures or failure to follow procedures.

Thomas Duke reported similar results in his analysis of twenty-one turbojet accidents (1991). Lack of procedural behavior accounted for 69% of crew errors – more than three times greater than decision-making errors. Duke supported his findings by citing several major accidents:

- NWA 255 attempted a takeoff with flaps up. This tragic accident killed 154 people. Cecelia Crocker, a four-year-old girl, was the lone survivor.
- Delta 1141 attempted a takeoff with flaps up (this accident and its lessons learned will be covered in detail in Chapter 5).
- US Air Flight 5050 ran off the runway at LaGuardia following the incorrect setting of the rudder trim.

These three accidents determined that pilots were not following procedures. But the more important question was, "**why** were pilots not following procedures?"

Deviation from procedures was first noticed in 1990, just twelve years after deregulation. The commercial aviation industry was rapidly expanding and growing through mergers and acquisitions. The executives from these newly formed larger companies were busy combining route structures, flight schedules, station operations, different aircraft types, and most importantly, cultures, into one company. While all of these activities were occurring, the frontline worker was working under an umbrella of different aircraft manuals, different operating manuals, different equipment, and different corporate policies/philosophies based on their original-hire company. This operational ambiguity created sloppy execution and a new term was coined called **procedural drift.** To prevent procedural drift within the airline operating system the solution was step-by-step procedures governed by corporate standardization.

> Procedural drift occurs when work becomes routine for a worker, the more apt the worker is to drift from the original/mentored way of conducting work.

Standardization departments improved step-by-step procedures and checklists; best practices were institutionalized; and a commitment to procedural discipline was communicated. This evolution delivered a procedurally compliant workforce.

One last change defined 3rd generation CRM. It was the addition of flight attendants into the CRM courses. This demonstrated the importance of CRM between employee groups and that the program was even more effective with everyone trained in this skill set. 3rd generation CRM not only expanded the involvement of other work groups but delivered procedural discipline in order to protect lives like that of four-year-old Cecilia Crocker.

4th Generation CRM

With CRM courses, an improved accident record, and standardization in place, the industry took another step change in safety. This step change involved creating realistic training in the simulator.

Here's how the Advance Qualification Program (AQP) changed the airline industry. In the 1990s, the airline industry was training their pilots in a program called Appendix H. Appendix H training consisted of a list of maneuvers that required each pilot to demonstrate proficiency in a simulator. It was a "check the box" exercise. For example, every nine months a pilot would attend refresher training and fly a pre-determined set of maneuvers. The list never changed and was therefore, standard. They flew events such as:

- Single engine landing;
- V1 cut (engine failure at rotation);
- Rejected takeoff at high speeds; and
- 15-knot daytime crosswind landing.

But these simulator events don't occur like they do in real life out on the line. So, the industry needed to adjust their simulator training in order to match the real world environment. They evaluated pilots on how they flew their procedures but began to evaluate CRM principles while crews were under a high workload. AQP blended the requirement to evaluate flying skills with the core principles of CRM (especially decision-making) while in the simulator – a successful formula to lower the accident rate.

At the end of the simulator session, a debrief was conducted that focused heavily on CRM principles and not on how the actual procedure was flown. This was an acknowledgement of the true underlying cause of the industry accidents – human factors.

5th Generation CRM

Corporate leadership was finally beginning to understand that blaming pilots for mishaps wasn't preventing the next accident. The acknowledgement that pilots (human) are not perfect has created what is now called "Threat Error Management" (TEM).

Threat Error Management has the advantage of two key supporting programs that has produced a wealth of human error information from which corporations can learn. The first program is known as the Line Orientated Safety Audit (LOSA). LOSA was designed such that frontline workers can be observed performing work in their work environment versus in a simulator. The results aren't about who made the mistake. Instead they are about how and why the defenses failed. LOSA is key in recording threats to airline crews in their operating environment and developing systematic solutions to them.

But a second key program that had been initiated decades ago would slowly evolve and begin to provide key learnings regarding human error to corporate leadership.

In 1975, a tragic airline accident occurred in Virginia. The investigation uncovered routine errors while flying into Washington Dulles Airport. But these errors didn't change other corporate systems or the FAA operating system. So these near misses continued until the fatal flight of TWA 514 (more about TWA 514 in Chapter 7). Out of this accident, a corrective action was a program called Aviation Safety Action Program (ASAP). Forty years later, ASAP is responsible for the incredible insight each airline has on how pilots make errors in the cockpit. One highlight from this program is the tremendous trust from the employee group – trust that corporate headquarters will use their openness in reporting errors to identify potential precursors to prevent accidents, not to lay blame. ASAP delivered a **Just Culture.**

> A Just Culture is an atmosphere of trust in which people are encour-aged (even rewarded) for providing essential safety-related information. They are also clear about where the line must be drawn between acceptable and unacceptable behaviors. (Reason 1997)

ASAP taught the airlines that that human error is universal, unavoidable, and a valuable source of information. CRM courses shifted to become a set of error countermeasures with three lines of defense:

- The avoidance of error;
- The trapping of errors; and
- Mitigating the consequences of those errors that occur and are not trapped.

Four decades ago, organizational safety changes were driven by accident/ incident investigation. Today, airlines deal proactively with accident and incident precursors from programs such as LOSA and ASAP.

What started out as an academic class – a class on psychology – called Cockpit Resource Management, has grown into an acceptance of how workers make mistakes during routine work. With this understanding of pilot error, corporate leaders develop countermeasures to address and eliminate these risks. Threat Error Management is an overarching safety concept regarding operations and human performance and is the operating foundation of an airline corporate safety system. The success of this evolution is undeniable. It has been proven that it is far riskier to walk on a sidewalk and be attacked by a dog than to sit in a U.S. commercial airline seat.

References:

Blake, Robert R., and Mouton, Jane S. 1994. *The Managerial Grid.* Houston: Gulf Publishing Co.

Duke, Thomas A. 1991. "Just What are Flight Crew Errors?" *Flight Safety Digest* 10:7:1-15.

Haynes, Al, Captain of UAL 232 – personal interview.

Helmreich, Robert L., Merritt, Ashleigh C., and Wilhelm, John A. 1999. "The Evolution of Crew Resource Management Training in Commercial Aviation." *International Journal of Aviation Psychology* 1:19-32.

Lautman, L; Gallimore, P.L. "Control of the Crew Caused Accident: Results of a 12-operator survey." *Boeing Airliner* (April-June 1987): 1-6.

Reason, James A. 1990. *Human Error.* New York: Cambridge University Press.

Reason, James A. (1997) *Managing the Risks of Organisational Accidents.* Burlington, VT: Ashgate Publishing.

3

Step-by-Step Procedures

"Quality is not an act. It is a habit."
Aristotle

In 343 B.C., Aristotle was appointed the head of the Royal Academy in Greece. While in this position, he counseled Alexander the Great and was the expert on subjects that spanned from physics to zoology. Aristotle was an intensely concrete and practical philosopher. He relied heavily upon sensory observation as a starting-point for philosophical reflection. His focus and drive created high situational awareness. Aristotle was known within the philosophical arena to attempt to develop a coherent system of thought by developing a common methodology that would serve equally well as the procedure for learning about any discipline – standards. Aristotle understood the power of detailed step-by-step procedures to deliver high operational reliability.

Today, frontline workers' habits are developed through two methods. They are built from day-to-day learnings (tribal knowledge) or through detailed step-by-step procedures reinforced by training (System 1). Habits developed through tribal knowledge are exposed to poor leadership, short cuts, and assumptions in execution that deliver the same accidents within the safety system. They deliver poor quality.

Use of step-by-step procedures to develop highly efficient safe habits will deliver high quality – operational excellence. When step-by-step procedures are governed by standardization, they deliver system quality, not just individual quality. For the airlines, the evolution of the importance of step-by-step procedures, governed by standardization to deliver quality, came at the expense of learning from accidents like Delta 191.

Even non-aviation enthusiasts know that thunderstorms are powerful. The energy that is released by one thunderstorm equates to the energy that was released by the atomic bomb on Hiroshima. Pilots are keenly aware of this power. Since

> A hazard is any source of potential damage, harm, or adverse health effects to someone or your safety system.

1970, the NTSB has identified low-altitude windshear from thunderstorms as a cause or contributing factor in eighteen accidents involving commercial passenger airplanes. Eleven of these accidents were nonfatal, but the other seven resulted in the cumulative loss of 575 lives. Thunderstorms are a well-known **hazard** to aviation.

Safety systems are designed around risk and risk is the likelihood or probability that a person may be harmed if exposed to the identified hazards. The National Climate Data Center (NCDC) has determined that Florida alone averages 100 – 130 thunderstorms per day. Thunderstorms are recognized for their raw power to endanger airplanes, and with a high frequency rate, this risk is elevated for the airlines.

In 1985, Delta Airline's corporate policy for thunderstorm avoidance was standard for the industry. It stated in part, that "when a flight encounters thunderstorm conditions, detour the area, if possible. When early evasive action is not practical, apply the following suggested minimum clearance distances to avoid areas where sharp changes in rainfall intensity are indicated. Below 10,000 feet, avoid areas by five miles."

On August 2, 1985, Delta Flight 191, a Lockheed 1011, was destined for Dallas (DFW) from Fort Lauderdale (FLL). The weather "guesser" correctly forecasted a chance of widely scattered rain showers and thunderstorms. The flight departed normally and was approaching New Orleans when Captain Ed Connors, a thirty-year veteran of Delta, requested a more northern route in order to avoid the tops of a line of thunderstorms that were hammering the Gulf Coastline. First Officer Rudolph Price, the designated flying pilot, accepted the new routing clearance and steered the large aircraft away from the severe weather.

During this deviation, the captain (the non-flying pilot) updated the weather at DFW. The digital readout of the current weather conditions at Dallas did not alarm Captain Connor. It seemed that the storms were clearing off to the east. The flight continued along the approved flight path and both pilots could see the weather continue to worsen to the south of their route. As both pilots chatted about the weather, Air Traffic Control vectored them further out of the way of the storms. These deviations placed them 120 miles north of Dallas.

Thirty minutes from landing, Delta Flight 191 left its cruising flight level for the descent to Runway 17 Left. While in the descent, Captain Connor asked Ft. Worth Center to deviate to the right in order to avoid the thunderstorm that was building up in front of them. All aircraft arriving from the east coast destined for Dallas were lined up in a conga line. Delta 191 was number fifteen in the conga line for Runway 17 Left at DFW.

While First Officer Price continued the gradual descent on a southerly heading toward DFW, Captain Connor scanned the weather ahead and commented, "I'm glad we didn't have to go through that mess." His reference was to the thunderstorm that was located slightly left of the aircraft nose but clear of the aircraft's track. The second officer looked ahead at DFW and stated, "It looks like it's remaining over DFW," – an ominous statement that went unacknowledged by the other two pilots.

Delta Flight 191, like all airplanes of that time, had a weather radar system that was primarily designed for en route weather avoidance, in line with corporate policy. With a minimum range scale of 50 nautical miles, the radar system was unable to detect windshear and provide detailed weather mapping. In essence, the pilots were flying blind.

Occasionally, air traffic controllers will send an all-points bulletin across the airwaves updating information to all pilots in order to pass important weather or airfield information to all listening aircraft. As Delta 191 continued to descend, the air traffic controller blasted an update to all aircraft, "Attention, all aircraft listening. There's a little rain shower just north of the airport and Dallas Approach is starting to make instrument approaches (versus visual approaches). Tune up the instrument frequency for 17 Left."

The Dallas Tower controllers were switching from a visual landing pattern to an instrument landing pattern. This change increased the workload on the pilots, but ATC's communication was an informative call to help all listening aircraft crews get ready for the new approach. It was a common and effective call to help build **situational awareness** – and a clue that weather was deteriorating at DFW.

Inadequate situational awareness has been identified as one of the primary factors in accidents attributed to human error. Thus, situational awareness is especially important in work environments where the information flow can be high and poor decisions may lead to serious consequences.

Descending through 7,000 feet, First Officer Price stated, "We're gonna get our airplane washed," an acknowledgement that the L-1011 was about to enter a rain shower. The Dallas Approach Controller asked the aircraft in front of Delta 191, "How's the weather on the approach American?" The American Airlines pilot responded, "As soon as we break out of this rain shower we will let you know."

The Dallas Approach Controller updated the weather, "We're getting some variable winds out there due to a rain shower." Flight 191 was number two for Runway 17 Left and fewer than ten miles from the runway. The cockpit voice recorder on Delta 191 picked up an unidentified voice that ominously stated, "Stuff is moving in."

One minute later and approaching seven miles from Runway 17 Left, Captain Connor switched frequency from Dallas Approach to Dallas Tower. First Officer Price brought the throttles to idle as the large L-1011 slowed to 150 knots (the final landing speed). Captain Connor transmitted,

"Tower, Delta 191 heavy, out here in the rain. Feels good." Dallas Tower responded, "Delta 191, cleared to land Runway 17 Left, wind 090 at 10 knots, gusts to 15." Tower's wind report wasn't strong enough to help push Captain's Connor decision to execute a "Go-Around." These winds were benign and offered no clue on what was actually waiting for them.

Captain Connor glanced at his onboard weather radar, set to the 50 nautical mile scale, and did not see any yellow or red radar returns that would indicate the severity of the rain shower. As the aircraft approached six miles, First Officer Price asked the captain to lower the landing gear and place the flaps to position 33 (the final landing flap configuration for the L-1011). Captain Connor configured the aircraft for landing and completed the "Before Landing Checklist."

The rain shower that the flight crew identified would later be called Cell C. However, behind Cell C and invisible to Delta 191's onboard weather radar was another cell – a storm that the NTSB would later label Cell D. Cell D was invisible to Delta 191's radar because of a known weakness of radar systems called **radar shadowing.**

A radar shadow can result from an attenuated signal from a nearby storm, masking a larger and more dangerous storm. The radar energy is unable to penetrate the first storm (Cell C) because of the heavy rain and downdrafts within it. Therefore, Delta191's radar screen was blank – indicating nothing was behind Cell C.

Through the study of information from the digital flight recorder, investigators determined that Cell D rapidly grew to maturity (in fewer than twelve minutes). Worse yet, Cell D occurred beyond the geographical confines of the DFW Airport's Low Level Windshear Alerting System (LWAS). In other words, the tower was blind to the rapidly changing weather conditions and so were the pilots.

As the large jumbo jet stabilized at 150 knots, First Officer Price noted, "Lightning coming out of that one." Captain Connor said, "What?" and the first officer repeated "Lightning coming out of that one." The captain asked, "Where," and the first officer replied, "Right ahead of us." The aircraft was passing 1,200 feet and four miles from landing on to Runway 17 Left. Lightning was a key, subtle indicator that a rain shower was maturing into a severe thunderstorm. The aircraft was fully configured to land when it began to rain hard on the windshield of Delta 191.

NASA and NOAA have extensively studied thunderstorms in order to improve the safety of the aviation industry. Through this process, they have discovered a significant event that is hidden within severe thunderstorms. It is known as a microburst. The term "microburst" was coined by Dr. Theodore Fujita of the University of Chicago. He describes a microburst as a downburst of air and rain that has a diameter less than four km (2.2 nautical miles). In essence, it is a localized column of sinking air that produces damaging, divergent, and straight-line winds at the surface. Once the microburst hits the ground, it will spread out in all directions.

Microbursts are not just dangerous to airplanes. In 2009, a microburst was the cause of the collapse of the Dallas Cowboys practice arena in Irving Texas that killed a worker. But for an aircraft that is below 1,000 feet, they are perilous. Here's why. As an aircraft is coming in to land, all pilots are flying a predicated landing speed for their type of aircraft (150 knots for Delta 191). This landing speed is slow and near the stall speed of the aircraft. When an aircraft enters a microburst, initially, the aircraft is hit with a strong headwind. Pilots will counter the headwind by reducing power to maintain their landing speed. Next, the airplane will enter the main column of downward air and the aircraft will lose its strong headwind and decelerate. In response, the pilot will place a little power back on the aircraft to make up the loss of airspeed. Typically, the airplane will bounce around a bit as the downdraft creates a turbulent environment, but the aircraft is controllable.

But here's the dangerous part of the microburst. The aircraft begins to exit the downdraft and flies into a large tailwind portion. This tailwind portion drastically reduces airspeed. When pilots notice the loss of airspeed, they will attempt to recover by adding power – lots of power. With the throttles in the full maximum power position, such a large loss of airflow over the wings can create an aircraft that is rapidly sinking toward the ground, even at full power. If the aircraft is below 1,000 feet, it could possibly be too late to restore the required lift generated by airspeed (more altitude is required to fly out of the stalled condition) and the aircraft can contact terra firma – Earth.

Cell D continued to grow, exponentially.

Delta 191 was passing 900 feet and within three minutes from landing on Runway 17 Left. The American Airlines flight in front of them had just landed safely and taxied clear of the runway.

Dallas Tower transmitted, "Delta 191 cleared to land on Runway 17 Left."

At this moment, Delta 191 entered into Cell D – the strong headwind component. Both crewmembers recognized the onset of the strong headwind that generated 23 knots on the airspeed indicator and First Officer Price responded to this headwind by moving the throttle levers to idle. This maintained the selected airspeed of 150 knots and the appropriate glideslope.

Both pilots had been trained to handle this situation and First Officer Price maintained his airspeed of 150 knots. Both crewmembers readied themselves for the upcoming down draft portion of the rain shower. Delta's corporate thunderstorm policy stated, "If below 500 feet above the ground and in wind shear conditions and glideslope deviation exceeds one dot below or above, a missed approach **should** be initiated."

Let's discuss policy statements for a moment. Flight 191 was just above 500 feet above the ground and First Officer Price had done a valiant job in maintaining the glideslope. Even if he hadn't, Delta's policy statement only indicated that the crew **should** execute a Go-Around. So far, this crew was compliant with corporate policy and in alignment with their training from their simulator curriculum.

Delta 191 was passing 800 feet and entered the rain shaft directly beneath the rapidly growing convective Cell D. Captain Connor cautioned First Officer Price, "Watch your airspeed." The cockpit voice recorder recorded the heavy sound of rain on the windscreen. Captain Connor correctly predicted what would happen next, "You're gonna lose it all of a sudden. There it is." Moments later, Captain Connor shouted, "Push it up, push it way up." Captain Connor was referring to pushing the throttles forward in order to achieve maximum power from the engines in recognition of the decaying airspeed. First Officer Price complied and Captain Connor was pleased with his rapid response, "That's it," he said. The L-1011 had flown through the head wind and the downdraft section of Cell D.

Passing through 600 feet and on glide path despite airspeed fluctuations of +23/-21 knots and downdrafts of up to 1,800 feet per minute, First Officer Price was still compliant with Delta's corporate thunderstorm training and was using superior airmanship to do so.

But now, Delta Flight 191 would encounter the tailwind gust portion of the microburst – an encounter that the NTSB would call severe and localized.

Within one second, the L-1011 speed decreased from 140 to 120 knots and a severe lateral gust struck the airplane. First Officer Price countered the gust with a full left yoke input and kept the aircraft in an upright condition. Simultaneously, he applied full engine power to counter the decaying airspeed.

But the localized and severe tailwind component of Cell D would be too much for the airplane to overcome. The L-1011 had entered into what is called a stalled condition.

Fully aware of this **stalled condition,** First Officer Price attempted to break the stall by lowering the nose two degrees while ensuring full power – the proper procedure. After completing the stall recovery procedure there was nothing more to do other than wait.

A stall is when the airflow across the upper wing surface ceases to flow smoothly and becomes turbulent, thus greatly reducing lift and increasing drag.

The L-1011 was at 120 knots and 420 feet above the ground. Delta 191's fate was sealed. With a rate of descent at 3,000 feet per minute (normal approach is 600 feet per minute), Delta 191 would land one mile short of Runway 17 Left. Moments later, the cockpit voice recorder recorded the first Ground Proximity Warning System (GPWS) alert, and the captain shouted, "Full power," – confirmation that the captain was aware of the weather and the energy state of the aircraft. Delta 191 emerged from the severe weather and First Officer Price visually acquired Highway 141, short of Runway 17 Left. He pitched the nose up to stop the excessive rate of descent. His last second maneuver prevented a violent landing, but the aircraft still touched down. The aircraft bounced and began to take flight again, but struck a car, instantly killing the driver. The aircraft then struck a light pole on the highway, causing a fire to breakout on the left side of the airplane in the vicinity of the wing root. The impact forced the aircraft to settle back to the ground in a left-wing-low attitude, careening toward and striking two water towers on airport property. The fuselage rotated counter-clockwise after the left wing and cockpit struck the water tanks. A large explosion occurred and the tail section emerged from the fireball, skidding backwards. It was a violent tragic ending to Delta Flight 191. Of the 163 passengers and crewmembers on board, there were only 27 survivors.

It's obvious that Delta 191 attempted to land at DFW in a thunderstorm under a corporate policy that instructed aircrews to avoid thunderstorms. But most investigators would have stopped the investigation here and labeled the cause as "aircrew didn't follow procedures." If you believe that this is true, then your corrective action from this accident would be to tell pilots to follow procedures. Case closed. But is that the **cause** of this accident? It's obvious that the equipment (on board weather radar) needed improvement. But why did this crew decide to continue to attempt to land in what became an obvious thunderstorm in the aftermath?

When the NTSB investigators learned of the presence of Cell D and the severity, along with rapid growth, they asked representatives of Delta if there was, "anywhere in Delta's program where they officially tell pilots not to take off or land directly beneath a thunderstorm?" The answer directly points to the underlying theme in this accident. The Delta corporate response was, "I think it's **implied**, and can certainly be **inferred,** that if we tell pilots to avoid thunderstorm activity by five miles below ten thousand feet, then that would be in that."

In order to understand the real causes behind this accident, the NTSB needed to know what influenced the **decision-making** of the flight crew.

> Decision-making is influenced by task factors, environmental factors and cognitive biases.

Could this accident have Crew Resource Management (CRM) implications like previous industry accidents, such as with UAL 173? The NTSB reviewed the condition of the culture of the cockpit. The investigators gathered the crew's training records, interviews regarding both pilots' professional reputations, and the cockpit voice recorder. The NTSB investigators quickly determined that:

- Captain Connor allowed a free and unrestricted transfer of information among the flight crewmembers;
- Observations relating to the weather were made without apparent reservation;
- Checklists were called for and completed promptly; and
- There was no breakdown in flight crew coordination procedures.

The NTSB correctly concluded that Captain Connor was a captain who willingly accepted suggestions from flight crewmembers. Poor CRM was not a contributing cause to this accident.

The discussion regarding washing the airplane is important. It suggests that the captain defined the current weather in their front windshield as a rain shower versus a severe thunderstorm. Furthermore, Flight 191 was one aircraft of many aircraft in the conga line of airplanes landing at DFW. One aircraft landed about every three minutes and none of the previous crews that flew through the rain shower reported any adverse weather – a powerful example

> Groupthink is the practice of thinking or making decisions as a group in a way that discourages creativity or individual responsibility.

on how **groupthink** (a cognitive bias) can affect team decision-making (System 1 weakness).

Next, the NTSB looked into the simulator training curriculum. Delta's curriculum included dealing with a windshear encounter for their crews during an approach. It reinforced Delta's thunderstorm policy by stating, "When encountering a windshear, the pilot should be prepared to apply thrust immediately to maintain a minimum of approach airspeed when encountering the windshear and to be prepared for a prompt reduction of thrust once normal target speed and glide path is reestablished." Interestingly, First Officer Price did exactly this. The investigators determined that the current training at Delta and in the industry seemed to advocate maintaining the approach airspeed and profile as the desired end result and *not escape* from the thunderstorm. The discovery of this nugget of information was key for the NTSB to make recommendations and prevent another tragic accident from happening.

The NTSB determined that the probable and contributing causes of the accident were:

- The flight crew's **decision** to initiate and continue the approach into a cumulonimbus cloud, which they observed to contain visible lightning (decision-making is a human factor subject);
- The lack of **specific** corporate thunderstorm procedures (significant finding);
- Lack of training for avoiding and escaping from low-altitude windshear (new procedures combined with training – System 1); and
- The lack of definitive, real-time windshear hazard information on board the aircraft (this would be fixed three years later with improved onboard weather radar).

This accident is a clear example on how **implied** or **inferred** corporate policies can fail the frontline worker without writing supporting step-by-step procedures, combined with training, in order to protect the frontline worker. Here's how.

Dr. Jens Rasmussen, a highly recognized system safety and human factor expert from Denmark, has studied the cognitive aspect of human error management for decades. He developed the hierarchy of human performance levels and defined them as skill-based, rule-based and knowledge-based. Within each performance level, he assigns an associated type of human error. First up is skill-based performance level.

Skill-based performance represents "sensory-motor performance during acts or activities that, following a statement of an intention, take place without conscious control as smooth, automated, and highly integrated patterns of behavior," in other words – routine work. For pilots, it is what we call stick and rudder skills – basic flying maneuvers. Biologically, we rely on our System 1 processor (automatic processor) to conduct routine work. Our System 2 processor (conscious processor) will be off. Rasmussen identified the types of human error that are associated in a skill-based performance phase of work as **slips and lapses.**

When the appropriate action is carried out incorrectly, the error is classified as a slip. When the action is simply omitted or not carried out, the error is termed a lapse. "Slips and lapses are errors which result from some failure in the execution and/or storage stage of an action sequence." (Reason 1990)

But thunderstorm flying doesn't happen very often, as avoidance is the "rule." It is not routine for anyone. Therefore, the crew of Delta 191 did not have a skill-based performance error (slip or lapse). The next level of human performance is rule-based performance.

Rule-based performance is when you are confronted with a situation where attention must be focused on making a decision or creating a solution. You must engage the System 2 processor. However, the situation is a well-known one for which the person has been trained. Therefore, as soon as the team identifies the situation (thunderstorm), the crewmember can easily apply a known solution (escape) and carry on with the original activity, often returning back to System 1 for routine work. Without a doubt, Delta 191 was in a rule-based performance scenario. It was just that the crew of Delta 191 did not recognize that they were in a severe thunderstorm.

With a clear understanding that Delta 191's accident was a rule-based performance issue, Delta would develop industry changing corrective actions. First, they defined the conditions for the new thunderstorm rule. They wrote, "Windshear procedures will be active anytime the aircraft is below 1,000 feet." The 1,000-foot limit is the safety margin (the cushion) and is based on science.

Next, Delta developed a solution that would aid the frontline crew with decision-making. Without radar, microburst characteristics are seen on cockpit instrumentations such as:

- Airspeed fluctuations;
- High rates of descent;
- High pitch attitudes; and
- Throttles at idle for excessive periods of time.

Delta's Safety Department translated the above conditions of a microburst directly to cockpit instrument indicators – easing decision-making for flight crews and breaking the effects of cognitive biases (System 1 weakness). In this case, the solution was written utilizing an IF/THEN format. Here is the industry-changing rewrite of Delta's windshear policy, translated into a useable frontline, step-by-step solution.

> Any time an aircraft is below 1,000 feet (just prior to landing or right after takeoff) and **if one** of the cockpit indicators indicates the following conditions:
>
> - + / - 15 knots airspeed;
> - + / - 500 fpm vertical speed;
> - + / - 5 degrees pitch attitude; and
> - + / - 1 dot glide slide displacement.
>
> **Then** the flight crew will execute a Go-Around.

No implied assumptions, no ambiguity (they removed "should") – it is a black and white solution. It delivers high reliable decision-making. Would this procedure have made a difference for Delta Flight 191?

Clearly the outcome would have been different for the crew of Delta 191. This solution (below) translated to cockpit indicators that removed **implied or inferred** to the frontline operator. It removed cognitive biases that were present that fateful day – a human factor solution that moved the industry a step closer to zero.

	New Procedure	**Delta 191**
Airspeed	+/- 15 knots	+/- 72 knots
Vertical speed	- 500 fpm	- 3,000 fpm
Pitch	+/- 5	+ 8
Glide slope	1 dot	1 dot

With improved performance from the frontline workers, engineers updated the onboard weather equipment as well. Modern aircraft now have radar screens that have fidelity within a five nautical mile scale and can predict windshear based on the characteristics of this weather phenomenon. Windshear equipment protects aircrafts by anticipating the high tailwind portion of the microburst and sounds an aural warning, "Windshear, Windshear," in order for the pilot to execute the windshear escape maneuver. This aural alarm makes the decision for the crew in the event that crews do not recognize the symptoms.

But in other industries, investigators would have faulted the pilots and labeled the cause "not following procedures." But rarely do investigators pull out the procedures and examine them in detail. Most corporations will have policy statements in place of detailed step-by-step procedures, which will make **implied** or **inferred** statements. Instead, it is, by far, easier to blame the worker for not following procedures than to explore why the frontline didn't follow them.

The third corrective action ensured that the airline industry would follow through on the new windshear rule and deliver flawless execution. In the simulator, pilots receive cockpit indications of fluctuating airspeed and large rates of descents – all of it done above and below 1,000 feet. The training program is reinforcing System 1 and System 2 decision-making. Once the pilot recognizes the condition by utilizing his System 2 processor, he makes the decision to Go-Around (eliminating cognitive biases that hinder effective decision-making). Once the decision is made, the captain's System 2 processor turns off and System 1 takes over for the Go–Around maneuver.

With corrective actions two and three combined, a **heuristic model** has been created that improves the airline safety system.

Heuristics are simple mental rules of thumb that the human mind uses to solve problems and make decisions efficiently, especially when facing complex problems or incomplete information.

But it's not just airlines that depend upon step-by-step procedures and training for high reliability. The overnight shipping industry does as well.

Long haul trucking is one of the most dangerous jobs in America. In 2012, there were over 317,000 truck accidents within the United States costing the economy $99 billion dollars (CDC 2012). The industry recorded over 700 fatalities. However, there is one company that had some of the greatest exposure to risk in long haul trucking that didn't record a single fatality. That company is United Parcel Service (UPS).

UPS is a company that delivers operational excellence while producing an exemplary safety record. On a typical day in 2015, more than 18.3 million packages were delivered by over 104,926 brown vehicles in 220 countries and territories.

With their drivers logging more than three billion miles per year, UPS can boast one of the safest driving records in the world. One of the company's drivers in his brown duds could be Thomas Capp, who has over fifty-three years of safe driving for UPS. Fifty-three years of safely driving his brown truck equates to over 2,000,000 miles. No doubt Mr. Thomas is a very safe employee for UPS, but it also shows that he is part of a very safe operating system; a reliable system. Mr. Thomas was awarded a patch for his 25 years of safe driving and he is included in the Company's Circle of Honor. He is not alone. Now, with over 8,703 Circle of Honor members, UPS continues to demonstrate that the system is producing safe driving behaviors that deliver operational excellence. In all, UPS averages one accident per one million miles driven – an unheard of statistic in long haul trucking. But how does UPS deliver operational excellence?

Almost all of us have used UPS. Personally, I've mailed everything from home loan documents to jet engines through their shipping system. They have never failed me. UPS's market capitalization is over $102 billion and they employ over 450,000 personnel. But the bulk of their operation and their safety record relies on those brown trucks that you see daily in your neighborhood. On average, a big brown driver makes 110 – 130 stops per day; delivers 200 – 220 boxes; picks up 40 packages; and drives approximately 120 miles. Packages can easily weigh over 70 pounds and driver success is measured by time, not safety! In other words, their system depends on rushing to get the job completed – extreme operational pressure! No doubt UPS hires quality people, but UPS doesn't rely on individuals to deliver operational excellence. Instead, UPS has created a **system** that delivers excellence by individuals.

Like the airlines, their success relies on detailed **step-by-step procedures** called the 340 Method. UPS developed its first driving manual in 1917. Through evolution, this manual had evolved into high reliable procedures by the mid-1990s.

> Step-by-step procedures aid workers by dictating and specifying a progression of subtasks and actions to ensure that the primary task at hand will be carried out in a manner that is efficient, logical and error-resistant.

For example, you don't just pick up a package any old way. You take 15.5 seconds to carry out "selection," the prescribed 12-step process that starts with parking the vehicle and ends when you step off the truck, delivery in hand. All the procedures are taught to UPS's driver candidates in two weeks of lectures.

The 340 Method procedures are so specific that they include everything from where to get gas (waiting for a station on the right side of the street reduces idling time and is safer than turning into oncoming traffic) to which finger to carry your keys on (hooking them on the ring finger puts the key in position for your index finger and thumb to turn it in the ignition and pull it out in one motion). It may seem fussy, but the driver is transformed by his muscle memory (System 1) into the "perfect" employee.

Efficiency in the package delivery business is important because just one minute per driver per day over the course of a year adds up to $14.5 million in inefficiencies (UPS website).

UPS drivers have mastered the techniques for safely completing their jobs with minimal physical effort and have lowered their incident rate – all while maintaining service commitments. These habits have become so ingrained into each worker that the essential methods of delivery and pickup have become an everyday habit.

Through eighty years of procedural compliance, the worker knows exactly how to conduct work. Procedures combined with training have pushed operational excellence to the seventh sigma level.

But job training, not safety training, is required in order to get high performance. In 2015, UPS invested over $800 million on training. UPS tractor-trailer drivers receive 80 hours of computer-based and on-road training before ever operating equipment. In order to achieve such superior reliability, UPS has continued to push learning with new virtual and augmented reality training devices that allow young people to learn in a world of video games and smart phones in order to achieve excellence.

Just as UPS, the airlines have mastered the value of step-by-step procedures, but it took the accident of Delta Flight 191 to highlight a hidden gap between corporate policy and a belief that frontline workers would execute on corporate implied or inferred policies. Fortunately, the corrective actions from Delta 191 delivered detailed, usable thunderstorm step-by-step procedures that still continue to deliver operational excellence today.

References:

Center for Disease Control and Prevention. "Vital Signs." *Trucker Safety* March 2015

National Oceanic and Atmospheric Administration, formerly National Climate Data Center (NCDC). *www.ncdc.noaa.gov.*

NTSB Aircraft Accident Report, Delta Air Lines, Inc., Lockheed L-1011-385-1, N726DA, Dallas/Ft Worth International Airport, Texas August 2, 1985

Rasmussen, J. 1983. "Skills, rules and knowledge; signals, signs and symbols and other distinctions in human performance models." *IEEE Transactions on Systems, Man, and Cybernetics* SMC-13, 3, 257-266.

Reason, James A. 1990. *Human Error.* New York: Cambridge University Press.

United Parcel Service. 2016. *"The Rise of Smart Operations: Reaching New Levels of Operational Excellence."* White paper.

4

Prospective Memory

"Almost all accidents take place because of human distraction."
Sebastian Thurn

As an adjunct professor at Stanford University, Sebastian Thurn has become a leading expert in Artificial Intelligence (AI). His company, based in Silicon Valley, is developing self-driving cars, automated homes, and smart drones. His drive to develop AI is based on eliminating accidents and making society safer. In developing AI, Thurn identified the most common root cause to human-caused accidents. It is how a simple distraction interferes with our workflow causing us to forget a critical step. That missed step is the start of the accident chain. Why distractions are so disruptive is due to our **prospective memory.** Prospective memory errors have been the root of major process/system safety accidents in all industries, costing thousands of lives and billions of dollars.

Prospective memory is simply remembering to perform intended actions in the future, or simply, remembering to remember. (Crovitz & Daniel 1984)

Artificial intelligence is not impacted by distractions, but humans are.

A distraction is what diverts attention or prevents concentration on the proposed task. Prospective memory is what we use to remember to call home, pick up milk at the grocery store, or to take prescribed medicine. Though the term may be new to you, all of us are very aware of our own failures regarding prospective memory. We just do little things to prevent it from causing major setbacks. Here's how: Microsoft builds alarms into our calendars that signal us fifteen minutes prior to a meeting so we are not late. Microsoft engineers understand that remembering to remember a meeting time is difficult for humans. Workers place yellow stickies on dials when the dials are inoperative in order to remember to not use the equipment. Pilots place checklist cards in awkward positions to flag a checklist item that hasn't been completed. High reliable people develop solutions to help them remember. Here's one of my favorites.

My wife is a flight attendant for a major international airline. Her passport is her livelihood. If she misplaces her passport, she will be displaced from her flight and lose pay, not to mention delay the departure of an international flight costing hundreds of thousands of lost revenue to the company. She protects her passport by placing it in the hotel safe along with one work shoe. One work shoe? As odd as it sounds, it's brilliant. She recognizes that one day she may be in a rush to leave and forget to remember to retrieve her passport from the safe. But with one work shoe in the safe, it's impossible for her to leave the hotel with just one shoe on. She has created operational excellence through the use of a forcing function.

This **forcing function** establishes a crosscheck to ensure that she will **always** have her passport (and her work shoes) and will never delay an international flight because she "forgot" her passport. Corporate leaders need to understand the importance of prospective memory, not only because of the frequency of prospective memory demands, but also because prospective memory failures have been devastating.

> A forcing function is a technique used in error-tolerant design to prevent the user from making common errors or mistakes. (H.J. Damveld, et. al. 1985)

On September 11, 1974, First Officer Daniels clicked the autopilot off and began to descend his Eastern Airlines DC-9 through 10,000 feet, inbound for Charlotte, North Carolina. All airline pilots are aware that when you descend through 10,000 feet, the flight is in the critical phase of work. The pilot's workload increases and mistakes during this phase can lead to catastrophic endings. It is time to be focused. It is time to go to work without distractions.

It is common practice for airline pilots to not use the autopilot in order to maintain their flying proficiency. Therefore, First Officer Daniels was hand flying into Charlotte. But not utilizing the autopilot would increase his workload management and decrease his situational awareness. In essence, he channelized his attention on the instrument panel.

At the Charlotte airport, it was a crisp, cool fall morning and it was still early – 0730. The calm winds and dew point created small pockets of fog in the tree covered countryside. The forecast predicted a beautiful day for the Charlotte area but the sun would need a couple of hours to heat up the air and burn off the low-lying fog.

Captain Reeves, an experienced captain and the non-flying pilot, updated the weather at the airport hoping that the visibility was good for a visual approach. The captain reviewed the weather report and learned that the visibility was 1.5 miles and the cloud ceiling was 4,000 feet. The fog was burning off, but from the cockpit view, the crew could see that North Carolina's countryside was holding on to small pockets of fog. Captain Reeves looked over at First Officer Daniels and joked, "I can't believe President Ford pardoned former President Nixon." First Officer Daniels replied, "I know."

Charlotte Approach interrupted Captain Reeves, "Eastern 212, expect the VOR (instrument) approach to Runway 36." Captain Reeves acknowledged the radio call from approach and returned to his conversation. "President Ford is beginning to take a lot of heat for doing that," he said.

Charlotte Approach called, "EAL 212. Descend and maintain 4,000 feet." The captain responded, "All right, 4,000 feet." First Officer Daniels, who had eight years of experience on the DC–9, continued to hand fly the aircraft to 4,000 feet. The final approach into Charlotte had begun.

Captain Reeves went on, "One thing that is killing me is all that is going on now with our country. We should be taking some definitive direction to save this country." Charlotte Approach interrupted Captain Reeves and called, "Eastern 212, turn to heading 330 and intercept VOR runway approach. Descend and maintain 2,200 feet." The captain repeated the clearance back to Charlotte and continued his conversation, but he was agitated. He said, "The Middle East is taking over everything. They've got so much real estate, so much land, and they bought an island for seventeen million dollars off Carolina."

The first officer continued to manually descend the aircraft to 2,200 feet and turned to a heading of 360. EAL 212 was directly lined up for the VOR 36 approach. First Officer Daniels retarded both throttles to slow the aircraft down from 188 knots to the final approach speed of 122 knots. The captain continued, "The stock market and the Swiss are going to sink our money; it's gold over there." First Officer Daniels replied, "Yes sir, they got the money, don't they? They got so much money." Descending and with the throttles at idle, the aircraft continued to race toward Runway 36, sixty-six knots faster than the target speed of 122.

First Officer Daniels requested "Flaps 5." Captain Reeves reached down and moved the flap handle to Position 5. With the flaps extended, the DC-9 continued to slow down. Captain Reeves said, "We are going to have to go back to owning just one car. If we don't get something going in our country, they'll own the world." First Officer Daniels replied, "Yeah."

Charlotte Approach interrupted their conversation, again, "Eastern 212, descend and maintain 1,800 feet. Cleared for the VOR 36 approach. You are six miles from Ross" (eleven miles from the runway). The captain acknowledged, "Ok, cleared for the approach."

As EAL 212 descended through 3,000 feet, the altitude alert signal sounded. Captain Reeves silenced the high decibel horn without acknowledging the alert and said, "There's Carowinds. I think that's what that is."

Carowinds is an amusement park with a tower that is over 340 feet tall. The tower is brightly lit by two strobe lights that flash with 2,000,000 candlepower. It is on aviation charts and anyone who has flown into Charlotte is well aware of it. The crew's discussion regarding Carowinds confirmed that the cockpit visibility was still good and the fog was below them in localized low-lying pockets – as predicted.

But First Officer Daniels didn't believe that the lighted tower was Carowinds. He said, "Ah, that tower? Would that be the tower or not?" Captain Reeves replied, "Carowinds? I don't think it is. We're too close to the runway to see it. Carowinds is back behind us." First Officer Daniels agreed and the flight continued 40 knots faster than the designated approach speed of 122 knots. And they had just passed Ross – the final approach fix for Runway 36.

The airlines safety system has implemented a tool, a human factor tool that builds situational awareness in order to prevent human error. It is called a **standard callout.** We will discuss more on standard callouts in Chapter 6.

For EAL 212, and for commercial airline flights in the 1970s, the standard callout plan started with what is called the final approach fix. For EAL 212, the final approach fix is called "Ross." "Ross" is identified on their approach plate (see diagram page 78) and is 5.5 miles from the runway. At "Ross," EAL 212 should have been at 2,200 feet. If EAL 212 was utilizing their corporate standard callouts, this is how it would have sounded:

> Standard callouts transfer unambiguous information between crewmembers and give confirmation that the information was correctly received. This transfer of information updates the crew's situational awareness, improves crew communication and promotes effective crew interaction during routine work activities.

Captain Reeves (when crossing Ross): "Ross."

First Officer Daniels: "Minimum descent altitude is 340 feet."

Captain Reeves (passing 1,000 feet): "1,000 feet" and would callout any deviations of airspeed/altitude.

Captain Reeves (passing 500 feet): "500 feet." At this point, Captain Reeves would continue to callout deviations of both altitude/airspeed until First Officer Daniels had fixed the deviations. (If there were no deviations – silence).

Captain Reeves (100 feet above Ross): "100 feet above."

First Officer Daniels (Based on whether he can see the runway or not): "Landing or Going Around."

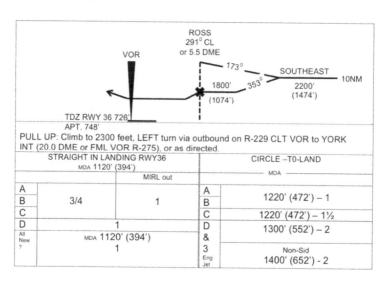

Profile chart for VOR Runway 36 Charlotte

When standard callouts go unanswered or a nonstandard response is given, the other crewmember is trained to ask again or to correct the callout. Improper use of callouts is the first sign that another team member could be losing situational awareness. Consider it a **"Stop the Job"** scenario. Neither pilot utilized any of the standard callouts for Flight 212. First Officer Daniels requested, "Lower the landing gear, please." Then added, "Carowinds is supposed to be real nice."

"Stop the Job" is based on the STOP program, a behavior-based safety program developed by E.I. DuPont de Nemours & Co. It is designed to prevent injuries and illnesses in the workplace by training supervisors to observe workers' actions and talk with them about both their safe and unsafe work practices.

Captain Reeves lowered the landing gear and stated, "That's what that is" (a reference to Carowinds). Captain Reeves began to read the "Before Landing

Checklist." As he completed the checklist, the altitude alert sounded (again) as the aircraft passed the altitude of 1,000 feet. Captain Reeves silenced the altitude alarm, once again. This alarm should have triggered a standard callout. Instead, Captain Reeves incorrectly stated the minimum descent altitude for VOR 36 approach – "394 feet." This was a designed crosscheck that failed on this flight. In fact, it was an opportunity for the first officer to recognize that the captain had lost situational awareness of where they were on the approach. But the distraction of the non-pertinent conversation had impacted the first officer's prospective memory as well.

EAL 212 was two miles past Ross and 400 feet too low, well below their minimum altitude for the approach. And both pilots were completely unaware of it!

Captain Reeves muttered, "Ross." First Officer Daniels did not reply to the scripted standard callout, nor conduct his crosscheck to confirm that they were at Ross. Instead, First Officer Daniels responded, "How about flaps 50, please?" The captain selected flaps 50 and EAL 212 slipped through 1,400 feet, 800 feet low. They were two miles closer to Runway 36 than they thought. At the same time, EAL 212 entered into one of the low-lying fog banks surrounding the Charlotte Airport. The crew focused ahead anticipating the acquisition of the high intensity runway lights for Runway 36.

Captain Reeves checked in with Charlotte Tower, "EAL 212 is at Ross." But this was not correct. EAL 212 was three miles past Ross and half way to the runway. Charlotte Tower responded, "EAL 212 cleared to land Runway 36. Winds are calm." Captain Reeves commented to the first officer, "We're all ready. All we got to do is find the airport." Moments later, Charlotte Tower spotted a column of smoke south of Runway 36 and the tower operator called EAL 212. There was no answer.

Eastern Airlines Flight 212 crashed 3.3 statute miles short of the threshold of Runway 36. Seventy-two people died. Only ten survived.

The NTSB determined that the probable cause of the accident was the flight crew's lack of altitude awareness at critical points during the approach due to poor cockpit discipline. The crew did not follow prescribed procedures – they did not follow the standard callout plan. Furthermore, the captain allowed non-pertinent conversations to become a distraction in the cockpit culture.

One advantage that the commercial airline industry has over other industries is the use of a cockpit voice recorder (CVR) or "black box" during investigations. CVRs have given investigators incredible insights into the final minutes of a flight. It records the squeaks that may indicate equipment failure, the tone of the flight crew briefings, and the history of the words spoken between crewmembers. It has become an invaluable tool for investigators.

When the NTSB investigators first listened to the black box of EAL 212, they were stunned. The investigators said, "EAL 212 reflects, once again, serious lapses in expected professional conduct." The lackadaisical approach to conducting critical work procedures was astonishing to the investigators. The recording from EAL 212 highlighted the insidious effects of non-pertinent conversations that become a distraction to a crew when conducting routine work – a distraction that shows how fragile a human's prospective memory is.

The crew's non-pertinent conversation caused both pilots to not perform their standard callouts – a callout that builds situational awareness through a crosscheck of their aircraft location to the approach chart or map. Flight Safety Foundation has recognized the importance of understanding our prospective memory by studying decades of aircraft investigations. Through hundreds of investigations they determined that the omission of an action – a simple missed procedural step – is the most common causal factor of accidents and incidents. And missed procedural steps start with a simple distraction.

In order to improve the culture of the cockpit and to limit distractions in critical phases of flight, the NTSB delivered a safety recommendation that would change the cockpit culture of the airlines.

The NTSB's recommendation drove the regulator (the FAA) to write U.S. FAR – Part 121.542 which states, "No command pilot and no flight crewmember may allow any other activity during a critical phase of the flight, which may confuse crewmembers from the performance of their duties or to interfere in any way in the performance of their duties."

For the purpose of this regulation, the word "activity" includes: "Engaging in nonessential or non-pertinent conversations within the cockpit and nonessential communications between the cockpit and cabin crews." The term "critical phases of flight" includes "All ground operations involving taxi, takeoff, and landing, and all flight operations below 10,000 feet, except when the flight is at cruise altitude." This is known as a sterile cockpit. And it works.

The NTSB report on EAL 212 highlighted the powerful and fatal impact of how the simple distraction of a non-pertinent conversation breaks down teamwork. NASA research, spearheaded by Keyes Dismukes (2006), noted that almost one-fifth of all major airline accidents can be attributed to prospective memory failures due to distractions.

But distractions to high reliable teams can manifest themselves in many ways, not just in non-pertinent conversations.

The airline industry understands that routine work places a cognitive demand on the brain – that simple, routine activity still requires effort from System 1. But new demands placed on the individual can exceed an individual's capacity. This can lead to newly presented information that may not be perceived or understood by the worker.

This condition is referred to as cognitive saturation and its occurrence prevents the accomplishment of further tasks. Even the act of ignoring non-pertinent conversation requires mental effort that may compromise safety. For example, while listening to Captain Reeves speak about politics, the first

Source memory confusion or misattribution refers to the ability to remember information correctly, but being wrong about the source of that information. (Harvard psychologist Daniel Schacter 2001)

officer may have fallen victim to **source memory confusion,** causing him to incorrectly believe he'd completed a procedure (the callout or crosscheck) when he had not.

But distractions are insidious by nature. It's not just the external distraction that can impact a crew. Internal distractions can have just as large an impact. Examples of internal distractions include divorce, family health problems, financial issues, or even a distraction caused by thinking ahead while working.

According to Chicago's O'Hare Airport's Annual Report, an airplane lands every 30 seconds. The airport is responsible for the handling of over 76 million people per year. It is the fourth busiest airport in the world and the air traffic controllers are considered the "best-of-the-best." During slow periods of arrivals in good weather, their work is considered routine. In my decades of flying, Chicago Air Traffic Controllers are considered the "best of the best". But even the "best-of-the-best" are human. Even they are susceptible to a simple distraction.

It was a calm, quiet Sunday night at O'Hare International Airport (ORD). The arrival air traffic was moderate. The south air traffic controller was responsible for aircraft landing and departing Runway 14R and departing Runway 27L. The flight crew of an Atlas 747 (call sign Giant 6972) made initial contact with the O'Hare south air traffic controller and said, "Hello, O'Hare Tower. Giant 6972 heavy, 9 miles from Runway 14 Right." The tower controller replied, "Giant 6972, O'Hare Tower. Runway 14 Right, cleared to land. [Wind] 160 at 8 and we will depart traffic ahead of your arrival."

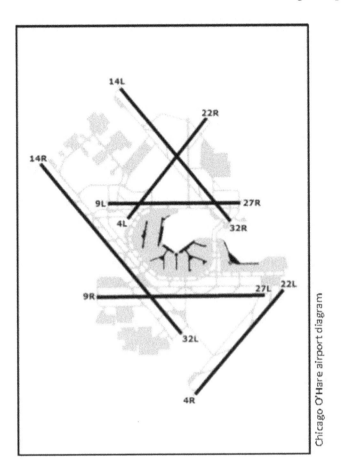

Chicago O'Hare airport diagram

Giant 6972 read back the landing clearance. In the meantime, United Airlines Flight 1015 was taxiing to depart from Runway 27 Left. During the taxi period, the flight crew of UAL 1015 was configuring the aircraft for departure. One important step in configuration is determining the weight of the aircraft. To do this, crewmembers wait for dispatch to send the passenger count, the cargo weight, and various other important factors. Once the crew receives this message, the first officer will enter the final weight of the aircraft into the flight management system and confirm the appropriate flap setting for departure. But UAL 1015 hadn't received their weights from dispatch and could not accept a takeoff clearance.

As UAL 1015 approached the end of 27 Left, the first officer switched frequencies to tower control. O'Hare Tower cleared UAL 1015 to line-up and wait. The crew of UAL 1015 replied, "Need about two minutes because of a delay." The tower controller said, "United 1015, let me know when you're ready. Hold in position Runway 27 Left." The first officer acknowledged the line-up and wait clearance and the captain steered their aircraft onto the runway. The south tower controller determined there was not enough spacing to permit a different aircraft to depart so he walked over to another controller and advised that he would not be departing UAL 1015 and would re-coordinate a release at a later time.

Air traffic controllers are very aware of the requirement for commercial aircraft to acquire their "numbers" or the weight of the aircraft prior to departing and have learned to handle these interruptions to their workflow. These delays can range from several minutes to over an hour.

UAL 1015's delay forced the south tower controller to readjust the departure rate in order to keep the required minimum safe distances between aircraft. So, he made a radio call and noted the delay for UAL 1015.

But the delay for UAL 1015 was only two minutes. The first officer called tower, "Tower, United 1015. We're ready, 27 Left." The south local controller calmly said, "United 1015, thank you. Fly runway heading Runway 27 Left cleared for takeoff. Wind 150 at 7." The first officer responded, "Runway heading, cleared for takeoff. United 1015." The captain powered up both throttles of his 737 and they began their takeoff roll.

At night, when you depart from Runway 27 Left at O'Hare, the windscreen is full of lights. The runway itself is black with one single row of lights indicting the centerline. At the edge of the runway there are white lights and beyond those lights are hundreds of blue lights marking the edge of numerous taxiways and intersections. And there are many aircraft taxiing or moving about the ramp. There's a lot going on.

UAL 1015 accelerated down the runway and the captain noticed a large 747 aircraft on the right side of their windscreen but on another runway. The aircraft wasn't parked, but moving at what appeared to be taxi speed. The UAL captain was unaware at this time but this aircraft was Giant 6972 – the one that was cleared to land at the beginning of our event.

When Giant 6972 was cleared to land, the landing clearance permitted the use of the entire runway. In other words, Giant 6972 **was cleared to cross the runway** on which UAL 1015 was accelerating.

As UAL 1015 accelerated toward takeoff speed, the captain concluded that they would collide with the large 747 at the intersection. The captain had no choice except to rotate early and hope he could become airborne prior to the collision of the two aircraft. So the captain smoothly rotated the aircraft 20 knots below rotation speed and paused, which prevented dragging the tail of the aircraft. As they paused to get airborne, the cockpit windscreen was full of an entire 747. Then, the captain pulled back to the maximum climb performance of the aircraft (23 degrees nose high). The 747 quickly vanished from the flight crew's windshield but they knew it was going to be close. There was still another 100 feet of airplane behind the cockpit that needed to clear the massive 747. Moments later, the crew realized they had cleared the 747, allowing the captain to lower the nose to an appropriate climb attitude of 10 degrees and fly the normal departure profile.

The NTSB determined that UAL Flight 1015 cleared Giant 6972, the 747, by thirty-five feet. Thirty-five feet!

The captain and the crew of UAL 1015 would later receive an award for their heroic decision-making and aviator skills. But this chilling event was all set up by a simple distraction during routine work – a distraction from planning ahead.

Distractions are so well known and tracked in the aviation world that investigators will hunt them down during investigations. The investigator doesn't want to lay blame on the employee but instead wants to understand the depth of how the human error occurred. Here's how the investigator accomplishes this task.

The south controller was asked whether he had any idea why the incident happened. He said, "Yeah. I let myself focus on something other than the basic air traffic control function of preventing collisions and started sorting out the efficient use of runways and airspace. I set a trap for myself by putting UAL 1015 in position when he wasn't ready, and when he did call, "ready," I was missing a piece of information and gave him clearance to takeoff." The south local controller said he simply forgot about Giant 6972 because of this distraction – the distraction of determining the departure path of another aircraft. He was thinking ahead.

He was asked whether he felt fatigued, overworked, or stressed out prior to the incident. He stated, "No. That came later" – an acknowledgement of another human factor that airline companies have learned to handle. It's called the **letdown effect.**

The controller was also asked whether the noise level in the tower was ever a distraction on the evening of the incident. He said, "Earlier that night, yes, but I wasn't going to be drawn in and removed myself from the situation." It was a brilliant response and an acknowledgement by the south controller that he was completely aware of the power of distractions.

> Our body activates its "flight or fight" mode during high stress situations and deploys chemicals like adrenaline and cortisol to prepare for the forthcoming challenges. After the event, those hormones disappear and the body goes through a period of fatigue. This is known as the letdown effect.

But other industries aren't as focused on eliminating distractions in the workplace. Instead they lay blame on individuals and refuse to accept that humans have limitations because of prospective memory failures.

I had the privilege to view five orthopedic surgeries in one day. These hospital teams utilized System 1 to conduct their work. By all measures, it was routine work. There were plenty of non-pertinent conversations during all of them and I learned that hospitals do not rely on the learnings of EAL 212 – a sterile cockpit.

In fact, hospitals measure the number of distractions during certain operating procedures. For example, the average total time of an operation is 111 minutes and the maximum number of interruptions and distractions averages 61. That's a distraction every two minutes during surgery. This study identified the major factors causing distractions. They are:

- Other personnel entering/leaving the operating room;
- Alarms activating;
- Phones ringing; and
- Non-pertinent conversations during surgery.

If you dig into the medical industry's safety record, it isn't enviable. The U.S. medical industry continues to leave towels and sponges inside patients' bodies approximately 39 times a week. But that's not the only issue. Wrong procedures are performed on patients twenty times a week. Wrong site operations are performed about twenty times a week as well and are the result of missed steps in procedures. (Makary 2012.) In all, the study counted 80,000 "never event" episodes between 1990 and 2010 that resulted in hospital payouts of about $1.3 billion. Death occurred in 6.6% of patients. That 6.6% death rate equates to 4,800 patient deaths from this study or in aviation terms – 67 Eastern Airline crashes per year! But the significance of understanding non-pertinent conversations hasn't occurred because the culture of the operating room isn't receptive. Yet.

The United States Marine Corps taught me that effective teamwork and communication have long been recognized as imperative drivers of quality and safety. And like most industries, healthcare is a team-based profession. The Joint Commission (2011) identified "communication" as the number one root cause (65%) of reported unanticipated events resulting in death or serious injury to a patient.

Similarly, surgical errors cannot be understood in isolation from the actions of other members of the surgical team. For example, D. A. Wiegmann (2007) determined in a study he completed, that teamwork factors alone accounted for roughly 45% of the errors committed by surgeons during cardiac cases – teamwork issues such as miscommunication, lack of coordination, failures in monitoring, and lack of team familiarity terms – the same four failures that were prevalent on the flight deck of EAL 212.

Several years ago I had ACL surgery. It was an unfortunate incident and I wasn't able to fly my fighter for three months. During the prep phase of the surgery, the doctor asked me what genre of music I wanted played during my surgery. I answered, "Rock, of course." It turns out they rocked Queen during my three-hour knee reconstruction. When I woke up, the correct knee had been operated on and I was on my way to recovery. But years later, when I learned the lessons of EAL 212 and the implementation of a sterile cockpit, I wished I would have had an opportunity to share with my doctor the importance of a distraction-free environment during the high risk phases of my knee surgery. In his domain, ACL repair is routine – he had performed over 1,000 ACL surgeries. In my domain, landing a jet liner full of 150 persons is routine. Perhaps I should have asked him what genre of music I should play when I am landing with his family in back of my airplane.

But it's not just about non-pertinent conversations. In a recent study on **noise** levels in the operating room, it was found that the average maximum noise level for an operation was over 80 decibels (dB), with absolute maximum noise level observed being over 90 dB (Healey et al., 2007). These maximum noise levels equate to sounds as loud as lawn mowers or the passing by of a subway train in an underground tunnel. Sources of noise in the OR are numerous and include the low humming of ventilation systems and other electronic equipment, alarms and feedback alerts on pumps and monitors, music from CD players or radios, telephones ringing, people entering and exiting the room, and sidebar conversations among surgical staff (Wiegmann et al., 2007). Noise can negatively affect anyone's performance. Noise can cause a distraction that hinders the surgeon's ability to concentrate by "masking acoustic, task-related cues and inner speech." In essence, surgeons cannot "hear themselves think" (Sanders & McCormick, 1993). Noise and distractions can also affect communication among the surgical team by reducing the ability to hear what others are saying or by causing statements spoken by others to be missed.

"Noise" is generally defined as auditory stimuli that bear no informational relationship to the completion of the immediate task (Sanders & McCormick, 1993).

To defend against prospective memory failures and their potentially disastrous consequences, professionals rely on specific memory tools or countermeasures such as:

- Checklists that are written using TO DO style formatting. TO DO lists identify when and where a worker will carry out a specific action. These checklists are designed and utilized when the workforce has time to read them and the speed of the procedure doesn't require memorization of workflows. Keyes Dismukes points out that having this kind of job aid has been shown to improve prospective memory performance by as much as two-to-four times.

- Understanding that memory is heavily influenced by cues built through training programs (System 1). Do not use checklists at your leisure. Instead use them during a pause of work execution.

- To overcome distractions while working with critical equipment, use the "say – look – touch" confirmation technique. This technique incorporates multiple sensory inputs and a higher level of task attentiveness is achieved. It also activates System 2, which has a very low error rate.

- Train crews to recognize when another team member is task saturated because a standard callout was not made.

All too often investigators approach an incident with a conclusion that the worker made a "foolish" mistake. They want to lay blame. Instead the investigator needs to dig deeper into the sources of external and internal distractions that disrupt our prospective memory. Then develop corrective actions that address how disastrous distractions can impact our prospective memory – corrective actions such as a sterile cockpit.

References:

Aircraft Accident Report, Eastern Air Lines, Inc. Douglas DC-9-31, N8984E, Charlotte, North Carolina, September 11, 1974, NTSB.

Catchpole, K. R., deLeval, M. R., McEwan, A., Paediatr, Anaesth. 2007. "Patient handover from surgery to intensive care." *U. S. Department of Health and Human Services – Agency for Healthcare and Research Quality.* 2007:17:470-478.

Crovitz, H.F. & Daniel, W.F. 1984. "Prospective Memory – A Brief Introduction." *Washington University in St. Louis*: Memory and Complex Learning Lab.

Damveld, H.J., Beerens, G. C., VanPaassen, M. M., and Mulder, M. 2010. "Design of Forcing Functions for the Identification of Human Control Behavior." *Journal of Guidance, Control, and Dynamics* Vol 33, No. 4 (2010), 1064-1081.

Dismukes, R. Key. 2008. *Prospective Memory in Aviation and Everyday Settings.* Mahwah, NJ: Erlbaum Associates.

The Joint Commission. 2011. "Improving America's Hospitals, A Report on Quality and Safety." *Journal of American College of Radiology.* 8:11;776-779

Makary, Martin Adel, MD. M.P.H. Johns Hopkins University School of Medicine. (Study Leader). 2012. "80,000-Surgical-Never-Events-Charted-Over-20-Years." *Health Leaders Media* December 21, 2012.

McCormick, Ernest J. and Sanders, Mark S. 1993. *Human Factors in Engineering and Design 7th edition.* New York. McGraw Hill.

NTSB Identification: OPS06IA008A, Incident on Sunday, July 23, 2006, in Chicago Ill, Boeing 737-322, 131 uninjured, NTSB

Occupational Safety and Health Administration. 2000. "Walsh-Healey Noise Standard." 3M Resource Guide.

Schacter, Daniel L. The Royal Society, "Misattribution, false recognition and the sins of memory." *The Royal Society* 10.1098/rstb.2001.0938

Wiegmann D.A. and Shappell S.A. 2000. "Human error and crew resource management failures in Naval aviation mishaps: a review of U.S. Naval Safety Center data, 1990-96." *Aviation Space and Environmental Medicine* 70(12):1147-51.

5

Checklists

"Name the greatest of all inventors – Accident."
Mark Twain

Mark Twain epitomizes the way most corporations learn. It may take an accident to drive change to the corporate operating system. Sometimes, this "reactionary" safety system approach will develop a corrective action that is so powerful that it shifts multiple industries and continues to save lives even today.

Within the aviation world, the "best-of-the-best" are test pilots. In fact, astronaut hopefuls are required to be graduates of test pilot school. For the Boeing Corporation, Leslie Tower was the best-of-the-best test pilots – and today's flight was to be one of the most important flights in Boeing's history. Captain Leslie Tower had a simple mission. Instead of taking an aircraft through the ringer to determine its flight envelope or weapons capability, he would perform a simple takeoff, flyby, and landing for a very important crowd. Nineteen members of the U.S. Congress had descended on Dayton, Ohio to see the latest and greatest experimental aircraft that Boeing had designed. This plane, Boeing believed, would change aviation history forever. In fact, Boeing's leadership team believed in this aircraft so much that it self-funded the project.

This was the day. Boeing and Captain Tower would demonstrate the capability of the next generation aircraft after five years of development.

With the lead test pilot flying the aircraft, it was time to wow the audience and convince congress to buy thousands of aircraft (and keep Boeing from going bankrupt).

Like all new test aircraft, this one was a giant leap forward in innovation. As Leslie Tower and his four teammates manned up the aircraft, Congress settled into the bleachers on the ramp to watch this impressive aircraft take flight.

This wasn't Leslie Tower's first flight in the aircraft either. He had been with the design phase, development phase, and had more flight time in this model than any other Boeing test pilot. Leslie Tower was the perfect pilot for today's flight. Everything worked like clockwork to get the aircraft to the hold short line. Loaded with experience and confidence, Captain Tower received takeoff clearance from the Dayton Tower controller and he powered up all four powerful, new engines. As Captain Leslie Tower turned the aircraft onto the runway, he applied full power to the new engines and the aircraft accelerated down the runway. This was the moment Congress had come to see.

On initial aircraft rotation, the congressional staff noticed that the aircraft lifted early and it looked like the tail was heavy. Once the aircraft was airborne, the aircraft rotated to the initial climb attitude. But then, it became obvious that something was terribly wrong. The aircraft nose kept climbing almost to a vertical position like a rocket. The aircraft's altitude peaked out around 300 feet where the aircraft ran out of airspeed, stalled, rolled over, and dove straight back to the runway in a violent crash. Captain Leslie Tower and Major Ployer Hill died on that tragic day. The three crewmembers in the back of the aircraft survived.

A devastated Boeing staff immediately convened an investigation to analyze what happened and to correct the cause. The investigation board determined the accident wasn't caused by structural failure or malfunction of flight controls, engines, propellers, automatic pilot, new flap design, or wing aerodynamic loading concerns. Instead, the cause of the accident was simple: a cockpit internal control that locked both the elevator and rudder was still engaged for takeoff. It was as if Captain Tower took off with the parking brake set. Pilot error!

The new and improved aircraft had such large control surface areas (flaps and ailerons) that on windy days these control surfaces needed to be locked down so that they would be protected and not bang around and be damaged. As Captain Tower prepared the aircraft for departure, he forgot to unlock this control lock and attempted to takeoff with his steering wheel (yoke) locked.

This accident ushered in the realization that modern planes were simply too complex to operate safely, even by the best test pilots in the world. If these highly trained test pilots could forget such a basic step as a control lock, the aircraft would almost certainly exceed the abilities of the average line pilot. Something needed to be created in order to prevent a similar accident. The only failure that day was the human – the pilot.

Boeing decided to create a tool that would jog the pilot's memory to ensure that all critical items were accomplished prior to takeoff. Instead of a team of engineers redesigning the cockpit and incorporating a **forcing function**, they created a simple fix that could be used immediately. This tool would be called a checklist.

> A forcing function is a technique used in error-tolerant designs to prevent the user from making common human errors or mistakes. For Boeing, they could lock the throttles when the control lock is engaged, preventing takeoff. Similarly in automobiles, reverse is locked out when the car is in drive mode.

Captain Tower's flight took place in 1935. That's right. It was over 80 years ago when Leslie Tower's tragic flight occurred in Model 299. Model 299 would eventually be called the B-17. When the engineers designed the very first checklist for the B-17, they didn't create a checklist with just a couple of critical items to jog the pilot's memory. The checklist contained 57 memory joggers. The length of the world's first checklist was an acknowledgement of how advanced aircraft had become and that the human could no longer rely on memory to be error-free. For Model

299, Leslie's Tower mistake would be Line Number 3 on the checklist. The challenger would say, "Control lock." The other pilot would respond, "Checked." (Historic Wings 2012)

I want to emphasize a significant learning opportunity from this accident. On today's aircraft checklists, control locks are still checked systematically by every pilot on every flight. It is a strong example of an industry that learns from errors and that Leslie Tower's tragic death will not be forgotten – better yet, never repeated.

The airline industry leads all industries in the development of and training related to checklists. Over the past 80 years, it has developed golden rules regarding them. One important golden rule is how to use checklists.

Most individuals understand the common checklist methodology of READ and DO. But as the industry grew in size, complexity, and in understanding of how humans make errors, it developed an additional technique called CHALLENGE and RESPONSE, where one individual reads the challenge on the checklist and another individual

> The Hawthorne effect (also referred to as the observer effect) is a type of reactivity in which individuals modify an aspect of their behavior in response to their awareness of being observed. (Monahan et al. 2010)

responds to the challenge question from memory. CHALLENGE and RESPONSE adds another layer of protection (compared to the READ and DO methodology) through the utilization of what is known as **The Hawthorne Effect.**

Once the B-17 checklists were issued and started being used by the frontline, crews discovered another benefit of checklists. It turns out checklists reduced workload. Checklists created more time to fly the plane and scan the skies for other aircraft, while delivering assurance that critical work had been safely accomplished. One by one, more checklists were added — not just for takeoff, but also for cruise, landing, and bombing. The idea was so simple and so effective that the checklist became the norm for an entire industry. I have decades of experience relying on checklists to trap my errors but it took a snowstorm for me to really appreciate their simplistic power.

I love snow. But snowstorms can challenge airline industry operations. Personally, I had flown thousands of hours but had never deiced an aircraft while flying fighters for the U.S. Marines. It wasn't that we couldn't operate our fighters in snow; we just avoided the cold climates when we could. As a newly minted Airbus first officer on a commercial aircraft, I would finally get my opportunity to deice.

It's not that I wasn't familiar with how to deice a commercial aircraft. In fact, it was quite the opposite. I had been fully trained on how to deice through a detailed curriculum and practice in a full visual flight simulator. But this first time event delivered a lifelong lesson for me.

The night before my three-day trip that started in Denver, the weather "guessers" had predicted up to eight inches of snow. It turns out they were right. The next morning we had six inches of snow on the ground with more on the way. I slowly drove to Denver International Airport (DEN) allowing plenty of time to arrive safely and on time. Once in flight operations, I printed all the required paperwork for the flight and waited for the captain. We introduced ourselves, briefed, and walked to our aircraft.

The aircraft had come in late the previous night so it was covered in snow and ice. I headed outside and went down the jet bridge stairs and began the preflight of our aircraft. Other than the ice and snow, the aircraft looked in good shape. I headed back to the jet bridge, entered the cockpit, and settled into the right seat. Since deicing is not routine work, I double-checked everything while setting up my cockpit. I found the deicing procedure in our manual and placed it within view for easy reference. It's important to note that we had a deicing **procedure,** not a **checklist**. Initially, some might say, "it looks like a checklist." But the procedure is written with simplicity in order to prevent human error.

We were ready for pushback and the pushback crew checked in with the captain. Everything was working just as in training. I received pushback clearance and we began to move backwards. For Denver winter operations, we deice on a special pad away from the gate. After we stopped the pushback, we started both engines and taxied to our assigned deicing pad. I shut down both engines. It was time to execute the deicing procedure.

Deicing is considered a non-normal procedure. In other words, pilots are not expected to have this procedure memorized because it is not routine work. This would only create errors which is why we utilize READ and DO as the methodology for conducting it.

We checked in with our deicing crew and the captain asked me to run the deicing procedure. I read the title of the procedure out loud. There are a multitude of types of deicing procedures and reading them aloud provides an opportunity for us to catch the mistake of using the wrong procedure. Here's the procedure for deicing our aircraft.

OFF GATE/REMOTE DEICING:

Prepare for deicing/anti-icing as follows:

- *Engine bleed switches* .... *Off*
- *APU bleed switch*.. *Off*
- *Pack switches* .... *Off*
- *APU master switch*...*As required*
  If deicing near the APU inlet, shut down the APU as soon as practical for best cooling.
- *Engines*...................................*Idle or shut down (as required)*

Procedure continues…

Did you notice that the procedure is written in the present tense? This reminds the reader that the READ and DO methodology must be used and that the reader should not use his memory to conduct this procedure.

Furthermore, the design of the procedure may also look different to some readers. It utilizes white space for each step. It evolved from a line-by-line style of writing procedures because of accidents that occurred due to fatigue or existence of poor lighting in the work environment. White space is about eliminating the mistake of skipping a step.

The captain had his deicing procedure out as well. Since I was heads down reading the procedure, I was exposed to channelized attention that narrowed my vision and lowered my situational awareness (System 2 weakness). With the captain reviewing my work, it helped him catch any potential errors while I read the procedure out loud. This crosscheck or oversight also improved the captain's situational awareness of the entire operation to prevent and trap human error.

I completed the deicing procedure and I announced to the captain that it was complete. He informed the deicing crew and they began to hose the aircraft down with deicing fluid.

Let's take a moment and examine another reason why this is called a procedure and not a checklist. Well-written, detailed procedures are built on lessons learned and some of those lessons are written into notes, cautions, or warning statements. Here is an example of a note within our deicing procedure.

Note: *Do not use APU bleed air for the packs until 15 minutes after deicing is complete. Air conditioning smoke/fumes may result.*

This note is very important to you, the customer. Have you ever noticed that the air conditioning system is shut down while deicing crews spray the aircraft? Perhaps you have reached up to increase the airflow on the overhead vent and were frustrated because no air was coming out. If the first officer or captain turns on the bleed air from the auxiliary power unit to the air conditioning system during deicing, the deicing fluid will be turned into smoke within the air conditioning system. Moments later, this smoke will pour into the passenger cabin through your personal vent. This is not condensation from a hot humid location. It is smoke. It has an odor to it. At this point, a passenger or flight attendant may incorrectly draw a conclusion that the aircraft is on fire and initiate an evacuation, when in fact, nothing more than some deicing fluid entered the system because a pilot pushed a switch too soon.

This note is not in this procedure because it **may** happen. It is in the procedure because it **has** happened. An inadvertent evacuation places significant risk to our passengers. It is cold and snowing, and our engines are turning. Our customers would have to jump out using slides to get away from the aircraft – not the desired outcome or the safest course. Airline operating procedures are the foundation to the success of the safety system. This safety system captures the cause of human error, formalizes the learning, and houses it in detailed step-by-step procedures – all through standardization. It is how the airlines pass on their lessons learned to all pilots and is a clear example of a vertical learning organization (covered in detail in Chapter 8).

The deicing lead radioed the captain and informed him that the deicing procedure was complete. We began the start sequence of the engines again and readied the aircraft for taxi. Since the deicing pad was close to the departure runway, it would be a quick taxi. I put away our deicing procedure, pleased that it went error-free, and began the next phase of our journey – the taxi. Yes, it was still snowing, but this was routine work and I had been in this environment thousands of times. The captain slowly and safely taxied our aircraft toward the departure runway while I conducted my **flows** in the cockpit. Once the captain noticed that my flows were complete, he asked for the "Before Takeoff Checklist." I grabbed the checklist and announced the title of it, the "Before Takeoff Checklist." I read this checklist utilizing CHALLENGE and RESPONSE methodology.

> Flows are memorized procedures that are designed to improve human performance based off science and how memory works.

I announced the first line of the checklist (Leslie Tower's lesson learned), "Flight Controls." The captain responded, "Checked." Then, I announced,

"Flaps." As I waited for the answer from the captain, I looked down to crosscheck my own work (Hawthorne Effect). To my horror, the flap handle was still in the up position. I immediately responded by lowering the flaps to the proper position for the takeoff. Since this "broke" the reading of the checklist, the captain said, "Go ahead and lower the flaps and when you're comfortable, re-read the checklist from the beginning." He said it comfortably and in a non-threatening manner. His only other comment was, "That's why we have checklists. All of us can make mistakes."

A little more background on the importance of flaps on an airliner – flaps need to be lowered to the proper takeoff setting in order for the aircraft to get airborne. Numerous airline industry accidents have happened because the flaps were still in the up position while a crew attempted to takeoff. It's not that the engineers haven't attempted to aid the human and prevent this condition from happening. In fact, engineers have placed a horn (a mechanical barrier) within the flap and throttle systems in order to alarm the pilots that the aircraft is in an unsafe condition. But if you don't have checklist discipline, then the operational redundancy in the system has been removed and your safety system is dependent on just a mechanical horn. Horns fail and so do people.

The captain's statement summed up the culture of the airlines. It's a complete admission that all of us can make errors and that we rely on a system of procedures and checklists to prevent and trap human error. However, I didn't let myself off so easily. This was more than just a mistake; it was a critical safety mistake that I should never have made. But I did, and more importantly, why?

Once we were airborne and the workload was low, it became obvious how I made my error. My routine was to always lower the flaps when we taxi from the gate. But today, we taxied purposely with the flaps in the up position in order to keep ice and snow from building up on extended portion of the flaps. My timing for lowering the flaps changed because of deicing. The deicing procedure disturbed my normal routine workflows. It became a distraction to my memorized workflows. But the airline safety system worked as designed. I relied on memorized procedures (System

1) to lower the flaps in order to be efficient, but in this case I failed. Importantly, however, the checklist (System 2) caught my mistake or trapped my error. It is how the airlines consistently deliver high reliability in a high-risk environment.

It is often said, "Checklists are written in blood." This is a true statement. In fact, the most effective checklists contain a CHALLENGE and RESPONSE to the critical phases of work that have killed workers or damaged equipment. These items are on checklists because of risk. But individuals aren't accountable for writing checklists. Corporations are. And corporations require standardization and training in order to deliver checklist discipline. In fact, if corporations aren't focused on standardization, then poor compliance will eventually lead to a system failure – an accident.

By the 1990s, deregulation had created an environment of rapid growth in the airline industry. Along with this aggressive growth came a clash of corporate cultures within cockpits. Yes, the frontline owns accountability for following procedures and checklists. But corporate headquarters is responsible for the culture. Gerard Bruggink, a well-respected National Transportation Safety Board (NTSB) investigator on human performance, highlighted the role of management on disciplined operations.

"An attitude of disrespect for the disciplined application of checklist procedures does not develop overnight; it develops after prolonged exposure to an attitude of indifference. Unless management first acknowledges its own role in the development of operational settings that provide errors, human error avoidance programs (checklist discipline) cannot serve their intended purpose in a practical and cost-effective manner." (Bruggink 1988)

Mr. Bruggink's comment is a precursor to the tragic outcome of Delta Airlines Flight 1141.

It was a beautiful morning in Dallas and the flight crew of Delta 1141 was looking forward to a routine flight to Salt Lake City. Captain Davis had over fourteen years with Delta Airlines and thousands of hours of experience. He had been a captain for more than ten years. First Officer Kirkland had over nine years with Delta Airlines and had been a first officer for about a year. Previously, he was a second officer, but that position did not give him experience flying the aircraft – just working the panel. The second officer was a recent new hire and had been with Delta Airlines for just nine months.

With the aircraft cargo doors closed, First Officer Kirkland completed the "Before Pushback Checklist." Delta 1141 received pushback clearance and Captain Davis directed the pushback crew to the assigned pushback spot. As the aircraft lurched backwards, Captain Davis requested that First Officer Kirkland start all three engines.

A little background on the starting sequence of a jet engine – during the start sequence the first officer has a very busy job. He scans the engine rpm gage for rotation, then engages the fuel lever, watches for ignition, scans the rate of temperature increase, waits for the generator to come on line, verifies that the pressure valve is closed, and checks the final idle speeds. The first officer must be ready to shut the engine down if the engine fails to start within parameters.

As First Officer Kirkland started the number one engine, he commented, "Did you pick up your pay check in Operations?" Captain Davis replied, "Yes, did you forget?" First Officer Kirkland responded, "Yes." He further continued the discussion by talking about making a down payment for a house. Chitchat, sure, but it set the tone for the flight and established the safety culture for Delta 1141.

All three engines were started on the 727. Ramp control needed to move an American Airlines aircraft before 1141 and said, "Delta 1141, give me a right turn, bring it between south ramp and hold short of the inner taxiway." First Officer Kirkland replied, "1141. Roger."

The American Airlines aircraft taxied past 1141. After waiting another minute, Captain Davis looked up at the control tower and commented, "How about looking down here at Delta now and then." The other two pilots laughed at the comment. The second officer chimed in, "While we are still young." The banter continued – the crew felt that American Airlines was receiving preferential treatment at its Dallas hub. After waiting three more minutes, Captain Davis asked First Officer Kirkland to shut down the number three engine in order to save Delta Airlines money – a common practice for the airlines. Delta 1141 continued to wait for taxi instructions.

Several other aircraft taxied by Delta 1141 and the captain commented, "We certainly taxied out before he did." The second officer read the "Before Taxi Checklist" and the first officer responded to the challenge questions. Finally, ground control (ramp) issued taxi instructions to Flight 1141.

Captain Davis inched the two throttles forward and the 727 began rolling. With a left turn, Delta Flight 1141 was in the long line of other aircraft waiting for departure from Runway 18 Left.

Delta 1141 began following other aircraft. The crew engaged in a conversation with the lead flight attendant who was in the cockpit, not in the cabin. For more than seven minutes, all four crewmembers discussed their personal dating habits.

As this non-pertinent conversation was occurring, Captain Davis continued to move their Boeing 727 slowly toward the hold short line to Runway 18 Left. Suddenly, Captain Davis asked, "Don't we have to be on ground frequency?" First Officer Kirkland responded, "Yeah, I'm sorry, I'm here talking with the flight attendant."

First Officer Kirkland switched radio frequency and checked in with ground control, "Ground, Delta 1141 with you on top of the 31 Bridge." As soon as the first officer un-keyed the microphone, he realized he made an error in his communication call. He meant to tell ground they were on the 18 Bridge not the 31 Bridge – a small clue that indicated a loss of situational awareness of the first officer. Delta 1141 slowly continued to creep toward Runway 18 Left.

Flight crews have learned that the departure rate for commercial aircraft is two minutes per aircraft. Therefore, pilots count the number of aircraft ahead of their position, multiple by two and determine how long before they will be airborne. This is how pilots determine when to start the remaining engine, read checklists, and prepare for departure in order to be ready at the hold short.

During this low workload period, the crew shifted their attention to a flock of egrets that were feeding in the newly cut grass surrounding the taxiways. The captain noted, "Egrets fly in after I mow my pasture." The first officer commented, "I've seen them all over the place here in Dallas." The conversation regarding egrets continued, then switched to a conversation regarding gooney birds landing on Midway Island. Birds were the focus of the conversation for the next four minutes.

The first officer keyed the public announcement microphone and said, "Good morning ladies and gentlemen. We're number four for departure. Flight attendants please prepare the cabin for departure." The first officer switched from ground frequency to Dallas Tower frequency.

Delta Flight 1141 was number four for takeoff and the captain asked the first officer to start the third engine. First Officer Kirkland reached down and initiated the start sequence for the remaining engine. The announcement of starting engine number three by the captain triggered the flight attendant to finally exit the cockpit and return to her seat in the cabin. With the engine started, the second officer grabbed the "Before Takeoff Checklist." Delta's checklist policy was to have the second officer read the checklist and the first officer to respond. The captain's role was to make sure it was completed – that's it.

With the checklist in hand, the second officer challenged, "Engine Instruments." First Officer Kirkland responded, "Checked Normal." Next, the second officer challenged, "Engine anti-ice." First Officer Kirkland responded, "It's closed." Suddenly, Dallas Tower interrupted the flow of reading the checklist and requested Delta Flight 1141 to exit their current position in line (they were number four) and to take position and hold onto Runway 18 Left. The first officer acknowledged the new clearance from tower and the captain turned the tiller bar to the left and powered up all three engines. The 727 began to pass the three other aircraft that had been in front of them.

The crew of Flight 1141 thought they had eight minutes until departure. Now, they had fewer than two minutes to ready the aircraft for takeoff. I have been in these situations as a first officer. Your workload went from light to maximum overload in a matter of seconds. Training consistently emphasizes to never hurry in these situations. Sometimes it is inevitable. But great captains (leaders) slow the workload down in order to ensure that first officers do not make any mistakes in these situations.

Three seconds later, tower said, "Delta 1141 cleared for takeoff, Runway 18 Left," inadvertently, adding more pressure to the cockpit crew of Delta 1141.

It is important for me to highlight the crew's next steps, as they will be the center of the investigation. The flight engineer resumed the checklist at the point where he had been interrupted. Not at the beginning of the checklist, but on Step 4. The second officer challenged, "Shoulder Harness." The first officer responded, "They're on." The second officer challenged, "Flaps." In a rush, the First officer responded, "Fifteen, fifteen green light." The two pilots continued the checklist and completed it as the aircraft rolled onto Runway 18 Left.

Without stopping, Captain Davis (the flying pilot for this leg of the journey) slowly, uniformly advanced all three throttles to the takeoff position. In less than a minute, Delta 1141 was rolling down the runway and quickly accelerating. First Officer Kirkland announced,

- "Engine Instruments look good;"
- "Airspeed coming up on both sides;"
- "Vr" (Rotation speed); and
- "V2" (speed).

At rotation speed, Captain Davis rotated the aircraft toward the standard climb pitch of eleven degrees with an airspeed of 160 knots. As soon as the main landing gear lifted off the runway, the aircraft stall warning indicator sounded. The stall warning sounds like a clapper and cannot be silenced until the aircraft's angle of attack is back within normal flight parameters. Captain Davis uttered, "Something's wrong."

Ignoring, or perhaps not hearing the stall warning indicator, Captain Davis continued to attempt to climb the aircraft away from Runway 18 Left. Two seconds later, there was a large compressor stall – the airflow into one of the engines had been interrupted which created a loud bang. Someone on the flight deck announced, "Engine failure" – twice. Captain Davis continued to pull backward with the yoke, reacting in the wrong direction per procedures. In reality, all three engines on Delta 1141 were working but suffering compressor stalls because of the high angle of attack. As the wing completely stalled, the aircraft no longer had the required lift to safely climb away from the runway. Delta 1141 was sinking toward the ground and the flight crew did not know why.

The 727 rolled to the right and within moments, Captain Davis correctly said, "We're not going to make it." First Officer Kirkland keyed the microphone, "Tower, Delta 1141…" He didn't finish his transmission as the 727 tail struck the instrument landing system localizer antenna approximately 1,000 feet beyond the end of Runway 18 Left. First Officer Kirkland keyed the microphone again, "Tower send the equipment." It was the last transmission from Delta 1141.

The aircraft broke up and stopped 3,200 feet beyond the departure end of the runway. The flight was airborne approximately 22 seconds and was destroyed by impact forces and a post-crash fire.

Of the persons on board Delta 1141, twelve passengers and two crewmembers were killed. The remaining 96 passengers and crewmembers were injured.

As the investigators swarmed over the wreckage of Delta 1141, it was evident that the flap system was not deployed prior to takeoff and quickly became the center of the investigation. Captain Davis survived the accident and during the investigation he incorrectly identified what he thought was the issue when he rotated the aircraft. He stated, "Both or at least one thrust reverser had deployed moments after we lifted off." He deduced his answer from the compressor stall that he heard upon rotation and the inability of the aircraft to climb. But he was wrong. Instead, he attempted a takeoff with the flaps in the **up** position.

But the NTSB investigators wanted to determine why he attempted his takeoff with the flaps up. So, the NTSB focused on Delta's procedures and checklists. Again, the cockpit voice recorder would aid in determining what went wrong.

The investigators went back to determine when the flaps should have been lowered according to the procedure (right after the engines were started). But the cockpit voice recorder identified a trend. The investigators noted that the captain did not stop the first officer's interruptions of cockpit duties when he initiated a non-relevant conversation with the flight attendant. Furthermore, constant interruptions and non-pertinent conversations occurred during the reading of the "Engine Start Checklist," setting the tone of casualness during the execution of a critical safety tool.

The "Before Taxi Checklist" was read and completed. Immediately after the taxi checklist was completed, the first officer began a seven-minute conversation with the flight attendant in the cockpit – a conversation that included each other's dating habits. The NTSB report stated, "Had the captain exercised his responsibility and asked the flight attendant to leave the cockpit or, at a minimum, had he stopped the non-pertinent conversations, the 25-minute taxi time could have been utilized more constructively and the flap position discrepancy might have been discovered."

The NTSB needed to understand why the crew read the checklist and why the checklist did not trap the error that the flaps were not deployed. The investigators looked deeper into Delta's corporate role in establishing the cockpit culture.

It turns out Delta management did not insist on a standardized approach towards cockpit management. They left that to the discretion of the captain. Testimony from management and training personnel confirmed that captains were allowed wide latitude in their conduct of cockpit operations. In other words, if non-pertinent conversations were going to occur, it was left to the discretion of the captain to manage them. The cockpit voice recorder indicated that the captain's approach towards cockpit management was passive and that he allowed events to materialize rather than firmly controlling the sequence of events. And this was an acceptable practice dictated by corporate policy!

Delta's flight manual backed up the passive cockpit culture. "The captain is responsible for the logical and timely completion of cockpit duties by the crewmembers. But it is the captain's responsibility to maintain the necessary discipline in the cockpit so that company procedures are carried out properly." In other words, the captain sets the tone for the working atmosphere in the cockpit.

There was no evidence that the intent, presentation, and execution of checklists at Delta were significantly different than at any other airline company. Procedures were in place that provided for an orderly execution of all required items such as lowering the flaps. The captain was required to ask that the appropriate checklist be completed and the first and second officers were expected to accomplish the items on the checklist or verify that they had been completed. But the execution of the checklist had become sloppy and both the first and the second officers recounted

> Normalization of Deviance is the working or mission environment created when established standards are subverted incrementally over time without consequence, by routinely rewarding shortcuts from the established norm. (Mullane 2010)

instances of responses to flap position challenges being given on the basis of expectations rather than reality. This had become the accepted norm at Delta. Checklists had fallen prey to **normalized deviation.**

CHALLENGE and RESPONSE checklists are specifically designed for the responder to reply with the exact or specific actual condition, not checked or "yes." They are designed to wake up System 2 and prevent normalized deviation. As a checklist designer, you want System 2 activated during checklist execution because it's the reliable processor; it catches our System 1 mistakes (forgetting to lower the flaps or a culture of normalized deviation).

This accident highlighted that the repetitive nature of checklist usage can be driven into the System 1 processor where most of our errors occur. It happens because the required response to checklist items is most often the same (flaps are usually set at position 15 for takeoff). It is very easy for crewmembers to fall into a habit of reciting checklist items from memory. Industries that do not capitalize on CHALLENGE and RESPONSE checklists to reduce risk will refer to this phenomenon as **complacency.**

> Complacency is calm contentment or satisfaction, especially when accompanied by unawareness of actual dangers or deficiencies.

For Delta 1141, it was apparent that the captain relied on the other crewmembers to verify critical cockpit activities, rather than monitoring and setting the pace of these activities himself. A failure in leadership for sure, but the captain never perceived a need to visually or actually check whether the first officer had lowered the flaps (a critical system). Instead, the captain relied on the professionalism of the first and second officers for the proper execution of their duties. There was no "**trust but verify.**" The human element was the single point failure in this accident and highlights how other industries solely rely on the perfection of their workers.

The investigators asked Delta employees, "Who in the cockpit would be responsible for verifying the flap setting?" An unacceptable variety of answers were given (captain, first officer, second officer) which highlighted the non-standardized approach to critical procedures within the cockpit. With this ambiguity, it is understandable that the flight crew did not know each other's responsibilities for lowering the flaps. In essence, the frontline employees worked with assumptions regarding critical systems.

The investigators reviewed Delta's operating procedures. It turns out, Delta's policy of delegating the maximum degree of responsibility and discretion to its flight crew was in large part responsible for other incidents – incidents that were caused by a breakdown in communications or a lack of crew communication. For Delta 1141, lack of corporate guidance culminated in a major mishap because the captain, the first officer, and second officer did not have assigned specific cockpit or work responsibilities. Nobody was specifically accountable for checking that the flaps were lowered.

In the end, the NTSB faulted the lack of standardization and procedural discipline in the cockpit to those who develop, supervise, and manage flight training and standardization programs. That's right, corporate was responsible for poor culture of the cockpit, not the captain! This learning was highlighted during the investigation when the Vice President of Delta's Flight Operations responded, "Many elements of our procedures are left to the discretion of the captain" – an unacceptable comment from a corporate leader that allowed for frontline ambiguity during critical job execution.

A NASA research psychologist testified after the accident about the importance of understanding **role structure** for workers. "With cockpit crews you would have a well-defined role structure – each job position being well defined and having specific responsibilities." A defined role structure

> NASA defines the term "role structure" as the degree and specificity of the structure of a group's activities.

significantly reduces ambiguity about who is going to do what and at what particular time. Role structure brings accountability and assurance to the safety system. Delta added role structure to their procedural manual.

A few years prior to fateful Flight 1141, the airline industry was in a ʼ͠d of rapid growth and mergers. During this period, the FAA learned ʼ͠nificant cultural differences, management integration, ͠blems. These issues were not addressed and :hanges to operating procedures, manuals, ams. Standardization was required in order ,ultures into one safe operating system. Delta delivered the importance of standardization discipline to the corporate operating system.

It was an accident for which investigators faulted corporate leadership not the frontline.

With an in-depth analysis of Delta's lack of procedural discipline, the NTSB needed to determine why the mechanical barrier (the horn) failed. The takeoff warning horn system on the accident aircraft had an intermittent failure problem that had not been corrected during the last maintenance activity and which manifested itself during the takeoff of Flight 1141. It was determined that the horn failed because of contamination or a misalignment of the takeoff warning system throttle switch – completing the final hole in the piece of Swiss cheese.

The NTSB realized that the checklist discipline problems noted on Flight 1141 were not isolated to just Delta. This accident was an exact repeat failure of another accident – Northwest Airlines Flight 255 in Detroit a year earlier. The NTSB observed almost identical checklist discipline shortcomings.

The NTSB determined that the probable cause of the Delta Flight 1141 accident was **inadequate cockpit discipline** by the captain and first officer, resulting in the flight crew's attempt to takeoff without the wing flaps and slats properly configured and the failure of the takeoff configuration warning system designed to alert the crew that the airplane was not properly configured for takeoff.

The NTSB had Delta rewrite their procedures and checklists to include the missing details of specific roles for each crew member – who specifically is responsible for checking the flap indicator before takeoff. Furthermore, Delta conducted a detailed study of frontline workers' workflows and standardized them. In the end, Delta removed ambiguity in operations. They removed assumptions in execution.

But the key instrument to change was the creation of a new departmer within Delta. It was called Flight Standards and even today, it govr all procedures and checklists to a higher level of operating detail. Standards goal is to manage the procedural language to en execution consistency and to avoid ambiguity. Flight Standar a "safety net" (a layer of protection) by managing procedures that prevent human error and checklists (crosschecks) that trap human errors.

But can detailed operating procedures along with checklists transfer to other industries?

My team was contracted by a client that needed a step change in operations regarding fracking in the Eagle Ford Basin in Texas. Our case study focused on measuring the success of the project through improving the misfire rate of perforating guns. Perforating guns are used to crack the rock underground in order to get oil or gas to flow to the well.

A perforating gun won't fire if the switches or electrical wiring become flooded with wellbore fluid (mud). This weakness in the perforating gun system was due to human error during the reassembling phase. Our client's misfire rate was 34 successful fires to every one misfire (34:1). Our team created three human factor checklists that took fewer than 90 seconds to read utilizing CHALLENGE and RESPONSE methodology. After 1,652 gun runs, the misfire rate had improved to 50:1 – an operational efficiency increase of over 47% and an instant savings of $200,000 **per** prevented misfire. This translated to a total savings of $18 million dollars for one quarter!

Furthermore, risk to personnel was decreased since fewer "armed" guns returned to the surface. Three years later, we reviewed the results of the checklists case study to determine if checklist discipline had taken hold. We discovered that the crews that were trained on the human factor checklists still used them and had an enviable misfire rate of 300:1. Crews that didn't receive the training were roughly at the same 34:1 ratio – proof that the simplicity of checklists built on standardization and employee training will deliver checklist discipline.

Most human factor checklists exist for operational reasons. But can human factor checklists be created for safety?

The Piñon Compressor Station is a small gathering hub in Colorado that supplies natural gas from the San Juan Basin to customers. A work party arrived to perform a pressure test on the facility equipment. The crew conducted a thorough toolbox safety talk prior to going to work. The contractor set up his pressure hose to the tie-in point and everyone left the buffer (safe) zone. A hose test was completed satisfactorily and the Pressure Relief Valve (PRV) was set to 5,500 psi. With a positive test, the contractor reset the pump to produce 5,200 psi in preparation of the next test. But the contractor accidently skipped a step in this routine procedure. The procedure was in the truck. The worker, who relied on memory rather than retrieving the procedure, should have set the PRV to 2,000 psi. (The pipe that was being tested was rated only to 2,000 psi). Furthermore, both companies' procedures stated that each time the PRV was set, it must be verified by the operator (a different individual). This verification step was not completed because it wasn't systematic – culture. With the PRV set to the wrong setting, the pump applied 5,200 psi to the weakest pipe (rated at 2,000 psi). With such a large overpressure being applied, the weak link failed and killed the contractor.

The investigation highlighted memory failure by the contactor as the cause of the accident. True, but memory failure as the corrective action is ineffective. After all, the correct action is to tell people to not forget. Our team recognized the similarity of Delta's 1141 mishap to this unfortunate contractor's accident. Our solution focused on designing a human factor checklist that would activate System 2 and establish a crosscheck of the critical systems when working with high pressure. We collected all the fatal accidents that have occurred while working with high pressure. Our research discovered 79 fatal accidents while working with pressure. From these failings, we developed a checklist that was written in blood.

Challenger	Responder
1	Exclusion Zones... "POSTED and ESSENTIAL PERSONNEL ONLY"
2	Valve/s Position... "CONFIRMED AND LINE WALKED"
3	Lowest Pressure Component.. "_____"
4	Maximum Working Pressure... "_____ psi"
5	Maximum Expected Pressure............................... "Expecting _____ psi"
6	Overpressure Protection Device... "_____"
7	Pressure set on Overpressure Protection Device.................... "_____ psi"
CHECKLIST COMPLETE	

When we introduced the checklist to the frontline, the response was immediate. They recognized the strength of this checklist and how it would trap their errors. They all agreed that they had made the same mistakes in the past and that this checklist would catch the highest risk steps when working with pressurized systems. Furthermore, it was simple, precise, and forced a crosscheck of the critical tasks that needed to be accomplished to get the job done safely.

Within weeks, the feedback was overwhelmingly positive. A field hand called us and informed us that the checklist caught a mistake and probably saved his life. Another company adopted the checklist and made it their corporate standard when pressurizing equipment. Now, the checklist has gone digital and creates a footprint of completion – delivering corporate accountability. Soon the checklist will be on augmented reality glasses, further reducing incidents and accidents.

How about manufacturing?

A manufacturing client contacted us about lowering their crane incidents at one of their manufacturing plants. Two years previously, they recorded 127 incidents while cranes moved their large, awkwardly-sized loads around the facility. We wrote standardized crane lifting procedures (flushing out assumptions) along with one human factor checklist (CHALLENGE and RESPONSE). The checklist was built from the root causes of all their lifting "dropped object" incidents. We returned to the factory, trained the frontline personnel and went home to await the results. Two years later, the company reported back to our team that the procedures and human factor checklist project lowered the number of incidents to just **ten**! Our standardized procedures and checklists delivered near flawless execution. But to show just how much the culture had shifted, our client measured how many times a checklist caught an unsafe condition prior to lifting a heavy object with a crane. Two years prior, their safety system recorded only six incidents of stopping the job. The human factor checklist delivered 49 incidents where the checklist caught an unsafe condition and stopped the job before the crane lift. This case study demonstrated a complete culture shift for the organization.

Checklists have been proven to be highly effective at trapping human error in the medical industry as well.

In the state of Michigan, Dr. Peter Pronovost introduced an intensive care checklist protocol (READ and DO checklist) that, during an 18-month period, saved 1500 lives and $100 million. According to Atul Gawande in *The New Yorker*, "Pronovost's work has already saved more lives than that of any laboratory scientist in the past decade" – a significant claim on the power of checklists. (Gawande 2007)

Checklists have evolved through 80 years of trial and error, have added simplicity to an already complex operating world and have saved millions of lives. To fly my aircraft without reading a checklist is like driving my car without my seatbelt. I simply wouldn't do it.

References:

Bruggink, Gerard see Delta 1141 NTSB report.

Gawande, Atul. 2017. "A Life-Saving Checklist: If something so simple can transform intensive care, what else can it do?" *The New Yorker*, December 10, 2017

Historic Wings. 2012. "From The Ashes of The Model 299." *Historic Wings Magazine* October 30, 2012.

Monahan, Torin; Fisher, Jill A. 2010. "Benefits of 'Observer Effects:' lessons from the field." *U.S. National Library of Medicine, National Institutes of Health* June 1, 2010.

Mullane, Michael. 2010. "Normalization of Deviance." Defined in *Hydrocarbon Processing* 89: 10:86

National Transportation Safety Board. 1988. "Aircraft Accident Report - Delta Air Lines, Inc.," Boeing 727-232, N473DA Dallas/Fort Worth International Airport, Texas, August 31, 1988.

6

Standard Callouts

"The difference between the right word and the almost right word
is the difference between lightning and a lightning bug."
Mark Twain

Mark Twain is one of America's finest writers. With his humoristic style and well-known books like *Adventures of Huck Finn* and *Tom Sawyer*, he mastered the importance of choosing the proper word at the proper time. His quote defines the spectrum of how one simple word can improve or impair a team's situational awareness. In any high-risk activity, words need to be spoken with clarity and brevity. Without high situational awareness created through communication, the team is exposed to human error and to catastrophic failure.

The essence of situational awareness is being aware of our surroundings and accurately projecting where we will be in the future. It is adaptable to everything we do in life and effective communication is key. In fact, the Flight Safety Foundation (FSF) determined that more than 50% of aircraft approach and landing accidents are attributed to pilots' loss of horizontal or vertical situational awareness. In other words, pilots thought they were closer or farther away from the airport than in reality (EAL 212 referenced in Chapter 4, is a prime example). Investigators determined that the leading cause of pilots' loss of situational awareness, even momentarily, was based on poor or no communication among team members. Therefore, in response to the FSF study and to improve safety, standard callouts were developed for critical phases of flight. (Flight Safety Foundation 1994)

Over the years, many standard callouts were written to cover critical phases of flight. But one specific work phase had measurable success – pushing aircraft back from the gate. That's right. One of the highest risks for the industry was pushing an aircraft backwards just two hundred feet. Here's how standard callouts solved poor situational awareness amongst pilots and the ramp crews.

Between 1964 and 1992, forty-six aircraft pushback accidents resulted in death or injury to a ramp employee (Flight Safety Foundation 1993). With the number of fatalities jumping to a total of twenty-one fatalities and with thirteen limb amputations in the last three years of the study, it was time to create a solution – an industry solution. In most of these accidents, the pushback crewmembers were actually run over by the aircraft during the setting of the aircraft brakes. A few cases involved tug drivers who were crushed as the aircraft taxied away from its parking spot. Investigations into these incidents identified that the pushback crewmembers who sustained injuries were required to remain in or near the hazardous zones associated with the aircraft. To create a solution, the investigators looked into corporate ramp training programs. They found that most ramp training courses were full of hazard awareness discussions and were delivered by On-the-Job Training (OJT) to qualify an individual to work on the ramp. This non-standard OJT training approach allowed for a large accepted variance on how to conduct work on the ramp – a variance that set up ramp workers for accidents. The NTSB summed it up best, "the sole reliance on human behavior leaves accident prevention exposed to such human frailties as distraction, concentration lapses, tiredness, poor understanding, and frustration." (NASA 1994) It was time for a solution.

The common ingredient in all of these accidents was either the ramp worker's or the pilot's loss of situational awareness of the other person. So, the solution had to involve increasing the situational awareness to both teams.

Standard callouts consist of commands and responses that are designed to enhance overall situational awareness of equipment, environment, and the people. First, a script is produced that contains the standard words that will be spoken. The words are defined to include conditions of the environment or equipment. When being executed, standard callouts rely on both parties to repeat the exact words from the script. If someone says something non-standard or no response is spoken, then both members know to stop the job, set the parking brake, and determine what is going on before moving the aircraft. Either condition indicates that someone has lost situational awareness and that teams must stop and update each other's position. With the development and training of the crews to standard callouts, the industry has enjoyed an enviable fatality free ramp since 1994.

The success of standard callouts on the ramp resulted in the development of more callouts in other critical phases. Today, if you peek inside the cockpit during an approach, you would hear this harmonization of callouts between pilots. It would be disciplined. It would be standardized. It would align both pilots mental model of work. It traps human error and delivers the right stuff. But if your team works without standard callouts, inevitably members of your team will work off separate mental models of what is happening around them. And all too often, a small distraction along with poor communication will end in tragedy.

It was December 29, 1972 and Eastern Airlines Flight 401 was scheduled to depart at 2130 from JFK to Miami International Airport. Captain Loft, First Officer Stockstill, and Second Officer Repo had over 50,000 combined flight hours. They were veterans of aviation. In the cockpit, there were two other people – jump seaters. A jump seater is someone who is authorized to sit in the cockpit but isn't part of the flying crew. These extra seats were designed to allow an airline regulator (FAA) to observe the aircrew using their operating procedures. So, when the regulator isn't sitting in the cockpit, the seat can be utilized by off-duty pilots hitching a ride.

On Flight 401, one of the jump seaters was a mechanic who rode in the cockpit for the entire flight. The other jump seater was a pilot who left the cockpit once the aircraft departed from JFK to sit in the cabin. The crew was flying a brand new Lockheed 1011 with no mechanical issues.

All ground checks and engine starts were normal and Captain Loft taxied the large aircraft out to the departure runway. As the captain turned the aircraft onto the runway, he handed control of the aircraft over to First Officer Stockstill. For this flight, First Officer Stockstill would fly the 163 passengers to Miami. With his hands on the throttles, he powered up all three engines and EAL Flight 401 was on its way.

At 160 mph, First Officer Stockstill gently pulled the yoke aft, and the aircraft lifted off the runway. During the two-hour cruise phase, the crew talked about what they received for Christmas and news about their families. Finally, with the bright city lights of Miami in the foreground, First Officer Stockstill gently pushed the yoke forward and the 1011 left its cruise altitude for Miami's Runway 9 Left. As EAL 401 passed through 18,000 feet, Captain Loft turned on the fasten seat belt sign and made the final descent announcement to the passengers. He called the flight attendants to ensure they had readied the cabin for landing. Passing 16,000 feet, Captain Loft checked in with Miami Approach Control who informed EAL 401 that the visibility was clear with light winds. It was a dark night in Miami – a dark, moonless night that created no discernable horizon over the Everglade swamps.

I am familiar with what it is like to fly during dark nights. I have flown off aircraft carriers at night with no moon. It is dark – cave dark. It is extremely difficult to determine the difference between the sky and the water.

In 1995, I lost a close friend when he lost situational awareness off an aircraft carrier in the Indian Ocean. He attempted to climb his aircraft to a higher altitude but instead he pulled his aircraft into the ocean – a tragic loss that reminded all of us how dark nights can steal your situational awareness. For EAL 401, tonight was one of those dark nights out over the Everglades.

First Officer Stockstill was hand flying the aircraft and smoothly leveled the large L-1011 at 3,000 feet. Once level, Miami Approach Control vectored EAL 401 onto the final approach course heading of 090. First Officer Stockstill addressed the captain, "Landing gear down, please." Captain Loft reached over, lowered the landing gear handle, and waited for all three green lights to illuminate. The aircraft slowed as the gear increased drag and the lights began to illuminate on the gear light panel. But this time only two of the three lights illuminated (identifying the two main landing gear). The nose gear light did not illuminate. Recognizing the unsafe condition, Captain Loft pulled out the checklist in an attempt to determine if the nose landing gear was down and locked. The first step of the checklist had the captain raise the landing gear back to the up position and then back down. In other words, he cycled the landing gear handle to determine if it was a loose switch. It didn't work. Captain Loft called Miami Tower, "Tower, it looks like we're gonna have to circle; we don't have a light on our nose gear yet." Tower responded, "Eastern 401. Roger. Pull up. Climb straight ahead to 2,000 feet and go back to Approach Control." The captain acknowledged the new clearance and changed radio frequency back to Miami Approach Control. The first officer leveled the aircraft at 2,000 feet as they overflew the airport, turning toward the west and headed out over the dark Everglades. Captain Loft checked in with Miami Approach Control, "EAL 401 is leveling at 2,000 feet."

Captain Loft instructed the first officer, "Engage the autopilot." The first officer reached for the autopilot switch and engaged it. The three crewmembers and the additional jump seater put all their attention on troubleshooting the nose landing gear light issue. The second officer performed a light test by simply testing the light bulb within the system. With four sets of eyes watching the test, the tests illuminated only the main landing gear lights – no luck on the nose gear light. But the outcome of this test indicated that it could be a light bulb issue and that the nose gear was actually down. So, the second officer speculated that the housing unit for the landing gear lights might be the culprit. The second officer asked the first officer to remove and reinstall the light bulb housing unit. Perhaps this would get the light bulb relit.

On the L-1011, the light lens assembly unit is slightly above and to the left of the first officer's left knee. With all four crewmembers zeroed in on the nose gear light, they watched in anticipation as the first officer bent forward. The first officer placed his fingers around the small, square housing unit and attempted to pry off the lens in order to access the light bulbs. Unbeknownst to the first officer and the entire crew, when he leaned forward, his right shoulder "bumped" the yoke. This "bump" disconnected the autopilot system and EAL 401 slowly began to descend toward the Florida Everglades swamps, unnoticed by any of the crewmembers.

In 1972, when the autopilot was disconnected on an aircraft, a light was the only indication that it was disconnected. For EAL 401, the autopilot status light was outside the view of the crew's channelized attention and went unnoticed by all team members. The first officer continued to fiddle with replacing the lighting assembly unit. As the frustrated first officer struggled, the captain sent the second officer into the electronics bay. This is a small compartment below the cockpit. On the forward wall in this compartment there is a window that allows someone to see whether the nose gear is down or not. As the second officer reached for the door, EAL 401 slowly slipped through 1,750 feet.

In the background, a soft horn sounded for one second and a light near the altitude read out illuminated. This caution light informed the crew that they had gone below the assigned altitude of 2,000 feet by 250 feet. But it went unnoticed as the conversation and focus of the crew was on the nose gear landing light, not the aircraft's altitude. The light would stay lit and unnoticed for the next three minutes.

The second officer lifted the hatch and climbed down into the electronics compartment. It was cramped and dark. He leaned forward and cleaned off the tiny window that looked straight ahead at the nose gear. But it was too dark out over the swamps to see if the gear was down and locked. Frustrated, he scrambled around the avionics equipment and climbed back up the ladder.

With the first officer reinstalling the lighting assembly unit, Miami Approach called EAL 401 and assigned them a new heading. The captain acknowledged the left turn and the first officer dialed in the left turn of twenty degrees into the autopilot system. The first officer believed he had placed the lighting assembly unit incorrectly back into the dashboard. He removed the light assembly again and spent two more minutes jiggling the lighting assembly unit to see if it would illuminate. He did not get it to light.

The second officer popped up from the electronic bay and in a frustrated voice announced, "I can't see out the window to see if the nose gear is down or not." He couldn't see because the captain failed to turn on the outside light which would have illuminated the nose landing gear and allowed the second officer to see that it was extended. EAL 401 continued its mild descent toward the swamps of the Florida Everglades.

But the crew wasn't alone. Someone else was crosschecking their altitude. The Miami Approach Controller saw that EAL 401 was now passing 900 feet. But in 1972, the culture within the aviation industry was one that considered the captain to be "god-like." So, the controller called EAL 401 and said, "Eastern 401, how are things coming along out there?" – a clear indication that the controller noticed the aircraft was 1,000 feet below altitude but the controller elected to not challenge the flight crew on their low altitude. The captain responded, "Okay, we'd like to turn around and come back in." Miami Approach cleared EAL 401 to turn left to a 180-degree heading. The captain acknowledged the new heading and First Officer Stockstill dialed in the new assigned heading of 180 into the autopilot system. As the first officer decided to resume his primary flying duty, he glanced over at the altimeter and saw that something was wrong. Startled he asked, "Did we do something to the altitude? We're still at 2,000 feet, right?" Captain Loft quickly turned his attention to the aircraft's altimeter as well and stated, "Hey, what's happening here?" In complete denial, the two pilots watched their altimeters wind down during the next twelve seconds from 100 feet to zero.

One hundred and one passengers and crewmembers died on EAL 401. When the investigators arrived at the accident site, it didn't take long for the investigators to determine that the nose landing gear **was** down and locked. With the cockpit voice recorder in hand, the NTSB investigation team focused on the distraction of the troubleshooting of the nose landing gear light and how it interrupted the routine procedures of the flight crew.

The investigators determined that the aircraft was initially flown to a safe altitude of 2,000 feet and the autopilot was engaged to reduce workload – a positive beginning to a simple non-emergency scenario. But the investigators noticed that there was no positive delegation of aircraft control. And the three flight crewmembers (and the jump seater) became so preoccupied determining the position of the nose landing gear, they forgot **the fundamental rule** of aviation – someone must fly the airplane. When the first officer leaned forward, the investigators determined that his shoulder bump was enough force (more than five pounds of pressure) to disconnect the autopilot. But the autopilot didn't sound an alarm loud enough for the crew to know that it was disengaged. After this accident, manufacturers would redesign the autopilot system by adding a high decibel alarm whenever the autopilot was disconnected – nowadays you can hear the autopilot disconnect chirp from the first class cabin. But the investigators needed a corrective action that would instill one of the most fundamental roles in aviation. It was solved with the creation of a standard callout procedure for stating who was in control of the aircraft during a nonemergency or emergency situation. Here's the simple but highly effective script.

When an emergency or non-emergency incident occurs, the captain will say, "You fly the aircraft and I will handle the emergency." The first officer will respond, "Roger, I am flying the aircraft." The first officer then looks straight ahead and focuses solely on the most fundamental aviation principle – fly the aircraft. Then, the captain will initiate the checklist/procedure. But the captain will read the procedure out loud in order to build situational awareness for the entire crew. There are no assumptions, no inferred roles during this critical phase. Furthermore, the first written statement on an aircraft's emergency checklist says, "Someone must fly the airplane." No kidding. A simple reminder of the most important task and a forty-year-old lesson learned that continues to keep the industry safe today.

To deliver 100% procedural compliance, the industry trained their pilots to the new callout standard. Furthermore, during the brief (tool box talk), the standard callout plan on handling an emergency is reviewed again. This briefing primes the crew's memory for flawless execution. It sets expectations. Standard callouts have systematically solved lessons learned from tragic aviation accidents but can they improve a team's situational awareness in other industries?

Deepwater drill ships exist for one reason – to drill for oil and gas into reservoirs that can be 35,000 feet into the Earth's crust, all while floating 10,000 feet above the ocean floor. It is a man-made wonder on which 200 personnel work together to bring us affordable oil and gas. At the heart of every drill ship lays the rotary table. The rotary table is where the drill pipe begins its journey through the water and then into the seabed. This work takes days to accomplish. By all definitions it is routine work – routine and dangerous.

When the drill ship is getting ready to "trip in the hole," the crews start connecting each stand of pipe together and run them through the rotary hole toward the ocean floor. Each 90-foot stand is waiting its turn to be retrieved from the derrick and brought over to the rotary table where the box section of the previous stand waits. The 110-foot derrick is built with two or three horizontal fingerboards whose purpose is to stabilize and hold the 90-foot drill stands in a vertical position. On the fingerboards, there are latches that keep each pipe in its designated position. Finger latches resemble a paddle and are functioned up or down when commanded to do so from the assistant driller. This latch is a mechanical barrier – the last barrier that keeps a stand of pipe weighing over 15,000 pounds from falling on the rig floor hands. Finger latches are a well-known weakness within the oil and gas industry and are the cause of numerous accidents when the finger latches open or close on their own – uncommanded.

On the new sophisticated drill ships, pipe-racking or unracking systems are used to move these large, heavy stands of pipe. A pipe-racking system's sole job is to reach into the selected fingerboard row and with three arms, grab the assigned stand from the derrick, retract the pipe from the fingerboard, and take it to the rotary where it will be inserted into the stand that is resting in the rotary table. At that time, a floor hand will connect (or torque) the pipe being held by the racking system to the pipe in the rotary table. Once the pipes are connected, the assistant driller will go get the next pipe. It's routine work for sure – routine and dangerous.

It takes a team of at least three rig floor personnel to complete this activity. For safety reasons, a floor hand is stationed two-thirds of the way up the derrick (60-foot level) and his job is to ensure that none of the finger latches are in the wrong position (down) while pipes are moved out. If a finger latch is in the wrong position, the heavy pipe will become stuck on the latch until the latch breaks and falls onto the rig floor personnel 60 feet below. If the finger latch doesn't break, the pipe will spring back toward the workers from the stored energy, possibly injuring or killing them.

The other floor hand remains on the drill floor and crosschecks that all the latches are open as the pipe enters or exits the fingerboards.

The assistant driller uses a computerized system to run the pipe-racking machine. His computer screen provides feedback on the position (open or closed) of the finger latches. It is typical that the three men are not always visible to each other but they stay connected during this orchestrated dance of heavy metal by using radios. The radio is the primary means to build team situational awareness of the operation.

Rig floor hands are a brotherhood and watch each other's backs with a relentless sense of pride. They are tight because of the dangers, remote locations, and the hard labor required to do the work. But they have not been introduced to the value of standard callouts during high risk, critical work. Therefore, radio chatter varies from zero communication, to "what's for lunch;" from haphazard finger latch status to critical information that needs to be passed on immediately. This haphazard, non-standard approach to communication creates poor team situational awareness. Poor situational awareness can be fatal.

It was another beautiful day in the Gulf of Mexico and just after 9 AM. The rig crew had been working for three hours and had connected 31 stands of pipe with no problems. Now, it was time to connect stand 32. The assistant driller commanded the pipe-racking (or unracking in this case) machine to reach into the derrick and grab stand 32. The pipe-racking system grabbed stand 32 and bit down on it for grip. The assistant driller commanded the pipe-racking machine to retract stand 32. As the pipe-racking system began to retract and unnoticed by the crew, a finger latch had fallen into the down position. As the pipe continued on its path back toward the clear area, stand 32 became caught on the down finger latch. This hazard was unseen by all three personnel (no radio callouts were attempted) and the pipe-racking machine continued to attempt to pull stand 32 toward the center. As the pipe struggled to be free, the floor hand left the safety of the green zone (safe zone) and entered the red zone (the hazardous zone) while stand 32 was still within the fingerboard area. He took a shortcut.

With lubricating brush in hand, the floor hand looked down and channelized all of his attention on the pin end of stand 32 – his target. As he approached the stand, the pipe-racking gripper could no longer hold the tension back. Within an arm's reach of the stand, the gripper head let go of stand 32. The lower end of stand 32 violently sprung back toward the rig hand striking him in the head. The blow killed him instantly.

This was a tragic and preventable accident. As the industry continues to engineer out the unreliability of the finger latches, let's review the accident with a human factor lens. First – one assumption about the floor hand: he was a good employee and wanted nothing more than be the best he could be in his job. Yes, he was new at the position but not new to the rig floor.

The investigation by the regulator for offshore oil and gas, the Bureau of Safety Environmental Enforcement's (BSEE), dived into the drilling contractor's procedures. They determined that the drilling contractor did not have a standard practice as to when a floor hand could enter the setback area (red zone)

A JHA/JSA is used to help reduce incidents, accidents, and injuries in the workplace. Each JSA has three elements to it: Basic job steps, potential hazards and recommended safe job procedures. OSHA during pipe handling operations. In fact, the drilling contractor relied on vague **JHA/JSAs** for job guidance for floorhands versus step-by-step procedures. This left ambiguity in operations. Furthermore, roles and responsibilities of the spotter were not defined and left to the discretion of the team – more ambiguity.

Next, BSEE reviewed the contractor's training program. (BSEE 2015) The contractor relied on OJT to teach their workers – same as the airline ramp employees of the 1990s. Furthermore, the drilling contractor didn't have documentation regarding whether the OJT was completed or not. For all practical purposes, the worker learned his job by watching others perform the same work activity (because of lack of step-by-step procedures) or he received verbal guidance just prior to working on the rig floor – a recipe for failure when working in high-risk environments.

BSEE's investigation correctly concluded that the death of the contractor was the direct result of him moving into the setback area and into the path of the pipe stand being held under tension when a latch on the lower fingerboard closed. A true statement, but the investigation needed to examine the system that failed that day and not the unsafe act committed by the individual. In fact, the drilling contractor's operating system did not systematically prevent employees or contractors from entering the high-risk area.

BSEE did discover that the victim reported the finger latches were open on the radios but that was it. His nonstandard radio call lacked conditions or environmental cues that would have prevented him from entering the red zone. Furthermore, there was no systematic crosscheck to catch his mistake of entering the red zone too early. A disciplined crosscheck would have stopped work if he entered the hazardous zone too soon.

BSEE's investigation noted that the drilling contractor lacked consistent training about when it was permissible to enter the red zone. Furthermore, the report highlighted that it **may** have contributed to the victim's decision to step in when he did. **May?** In my opinion, it absolutely contributed to this accident. The BSEE report noted that rig hands admitted that the movement into the setback area while the stands were being moved was not allowed. However, determining exactly when it was safe to move into the setback area varied from rig-to-rig, person-to-person, and shift-to-shift. This loose approach to conducting high-risk activities created ambiguity in operations. Ambiguity in procedures always delivers sloppy execution and increases risk – whether on a drill ship or the flight deck of Delta 1141.

All three of BSEE's recommendations would not prevent the accident from happening again. There's no systematic learning. For example, adding another line into a broken JSA system (a collection of tasks steps, hazards, and mitigation), reviewing an ineffective OJT program (lack of formal job training – not safety), or adding a derrick spotter without standardized communication will not change frontline workers' behavior. It will not prevent a similar occurrence.

Remarkably, the NTSB's quote concerning ramp fatalities from thirty years ago should have been entered into this investigation. "This reliance on human behavior leaves accident prevention exposed to such human frailties as distraction, concentration lapse, tiredness, and poor understanding." It's time to provide solutions that deliver the safe behavior in oil and gas. Handling pipe in the derrick requires standard callouts to reduce the hazard to zero.

Standard callouts in the airline industry were created to transfer unambiguous information between crewmembers and confirm that the information was correctly received. This transfer of information updates the crew's situational awareness, improves crew communication, and promotes effective crew interaction during routine work activities. It prevents fatal accidents.

It is important to emphasize that standard callouts are written as procedures, governed by standardization, and audited for improvement. Here is the one line of a standard callout plan that visually confirms the floor hand is clear of the drill pipe.

ACTIONS / CONDITIONS		CALLOUT
Assistant driller closes gripper heads, rollers, and guide claws. With a good bite and green zone clear of equipment and floor hand, the derrick spotter announces "Good Bite, Floor Hand Clear."	**FLOOR HAND**	**"Good Bite, Floor Hand Clear."**

The derrick spotter keeps his eye on the red zone ensuring it is safe throughout the operation. His callout serves two functions. It builds situational awareness for the entire team **and** detects departure from routine activity, triggering a stop the job action. This solution allows the team more time to deal with the unexpected – the deviation from what was planned.

All industries that require teamwork can eliminate human error by increasing the team's situational awareness through the implementation of standard callouts. This is especially true in the healthcare industry.

Estimates say that in the United States, thousands of people visit the emergency room annually because of allergic reactions to food. During those visits, 150 to 200 people die because of their food allergies. It is estimated that around 50% to 60% of those fatal cases of anaphylaxis (a potentially fatal condition in which sufferers have trouble breathing because of constricted airways; experience a sudden and drastic drop in blood pressure; and have an increased pulse rate and with a rapid onset, may cause death) were caused by peanut allergies.

Peanut allergies are the body's overreaction to certain proteins found in peanuts. The immune system's response to these allergens is to trigger an antibody which then triggers other chemicals. One of the scariest results of these chemicals is the chance for anaphylaxis.

The emergency room of a hospital is a high-risk, chaotic world where communication is key for high situational awareness. It is routine work in which workers use nonstandard communication to save people's lives. But nonstandard communication leaves room for assumptions during moments of crisis.

Ann Marie Fitzgerald Chase, a registered nurse, documents a familiar example of poor miscommunication between team members. A two-year-old child arrived in the emergency department crying, wheezing, and rubbing her puffy eyes. Her face was red and hot, and her eyes were nearly swollen shut. She had been dining out with her mother and somehow had an exposure to food containing peanuts. This little girl was allergic to peanuts. The ER doctor shouted, "Give that kid a milligram of Epi." The doctor correctly diagnosed the little girl's condition from two doors down. He knew time was of the essence and shouted the solution. The nurse responded, "You mean .01 milligram, right?" The nurse knew the order was incorrect and clarified the dosage. The doctor responded, "Yes, a milligram, you know what I mean." Once again, the nurse knew that the doctor was working with an **assumption** and that communication needed to be perfect between them, but the nurse disagreed and corrected the dosage again. She asked," You mean 0.001 g, of 1:1000 Epinephrine, is this right?" The nurse began drawing up the medication in the room, as time was of the essence. The child was in full-blown anaphylaxis and needed treatment immediately. A new nurse taking this verbal order for Epinephrine may not have questioned the order because it was an emergency or because the doctor was always right. If the original order had been given to the child she would've received a potentially lethal overdose. But with an experienced nurse who professionally questioned the poor communication, the young girl was given the proper dosage and quickly recovered. In these hospital circumstances, standard, effective communication can only be delivered through standard callouts.

The importance of standardization cannot be overlooked. A hospital per diem nurse, employed by two different hospitals, began her shift to find that one of her patients had gone into cardiac arrest. She responded quickly by picking up the phone and announcing "Code Blue." Within minutes, she was surrounded by security guards and police officers with weapons in hand. To her dismay, the nurse was informed that Code Blue is a security alert in this facility. In her other place of employment, it means cardiac arrest. The correct team was quickly brought to the bedside and the patient recovered.

With a focus on precise communication during routine or emergency situations, an organization will step closer to becoming a high reliable organization with the implementation of standard callouts. Standard callouts build a team's situational awareness of each other, remove ambiguity and protect workers from becoming another workplace statistic.

References:

Aircraft Accident Report, Eastern Air Lines, Inc. L-1011, N310FA, Miami, Florida, December 29, 1972, NTSB

BSEE Panel Report 2017-001. "Fatality During Pipe Handling." Investigation of October 20, 2015.

Chase, Ann Marie Fitzgerald, MSN, RN, CEN. 2010. "Team communication in emergencies, simple strategies for staff." *Zoll Code Communications* IV:2. April 2010.

Flight Safety Foundation, Airport Operations, Special Edition, May-June 1994. 20:3

7

Just Culture

"88 percent of all workplace accidents and
injuries are caused by "man-failure."
Herbert William Heinrich

Herbert William Heinrich was an American industrial safety pioneer in the 1930s. As the Assistant Superintendent of Engineering and Inspection Division of Travelers Insurance Company, he investigated thousands of accidents in order to give recommendations that would prevent similar type accidents (a reactive safety system). Over decades of investigating accidents, a common theme became obvious to Mr. Heinrich. He discovered a ratio – for every one major injury or fatality, there were 29 incidents that caused minor injuries and 300 near misses that caused no injuries (a 1-to-300 ratio). It became known as Heinrich's Law. The ratio is often depicted as an iceberg. If a company wants to delete a fatality (the one event), the company's safety system must ensure that the organization **learns** from the 300 near misses.

Years later, Heinrich's Law would evolve into Behavior Based Safety (BBS). BBS has been a successful safety program but it only identifies hazards in the work environment. BBS fails in that the system does not review reports of unsafe acts from the frontline worker. According to Heinrich's quote, BBS programs fail to learn from the 88% of the causes of accidents – unsafe acts from the frontline.

After talking with supervisors at accident sites, Heinrich learned that, in most cases, supervisors blamed workers for causing accidents. It was the fault of the workers and the supervisor wanted to fire or otherwise discipline them for their mistakes. Supervisors' behavior established a blame culture. Heinrich didn't have access to supervisors to educate them about the importance of learning from unsafe acts. Therefore, as an outside insurance investigator, Heinrich focused on the issues over which he had control – removing hazards such as unguarded rotating equipment, slippery factory floors, and loud factory work settings. Without a doubt, Mr. Heinrich's efforts were responsible for preventing thousands of life-altering injuries but he was never able to demonstrate how an organization could learn from the 300 unsafe acts. Forty years later, it would take TWA Flight 514 to identify a solution – a program where workers feel comfortable reporting their unsafe acts – and design a system of organizational learning that changes a safety culture to a just culture.

In January 1974, United Airlines began a new safety initiative called the Flight Safety Awareness Program (FSAP). The goal of United's FSAP Program was the same as Mr. Heinrich's – to learn from the 300 near misses caused by unsafe acts. A key element of the program was that the reporter of the incident would receive protection for making notification of the near miss. United's leadership vowed to vigorously protect the reporter's anonymity unless the reporter waived that protection.

In November 1974, United Airlines FSAP program would become key in an investigation. United's FSAP program received a near miss report that described how one of their crewmembers made a near fatal mistake – an unsafe act.

Here's what the reporter shared. The flight was descending to land at Washington Dulles International Airport. At approximately 40 miles from touchdown and at 7,000 feet, Dulles Approach Control cleared the UAL 727 for an instrument (VOR DME) Runway 12 approach. At the time the crew unknowingly descended to an unsafe altitude of 1,800 feet instead of the minimum safe altitude of 3,400 feet required for that approach segment. It was a close call because Mt. Weather's peak is at 1,760 feet (see diagram on next page).

A little background on United's approach clearance: In 1974, Dulles Approach received a new approach radar that vastly improved the tracking and ultimately the handling of aircraft in and out of the Washington, D.C. area. Without radar, Dulles Approach controllers could not know the altitude of the aircraft. Therefore, when Dulles Approach cleared an aircraft for the approach, the pilots were responsible for maneuvering the aircraft to land and were responsible for being at a safe altitude. Now, with sophisticated radar, Dulles Approach could clear an aircraft for the approach **and** provide altitude warnings to the crew in the event that they descended to the wrong altitude. The addition of radar to Dulles Approach added a new safety margin for commercial aviation and was an advancement in technology that would save lives.

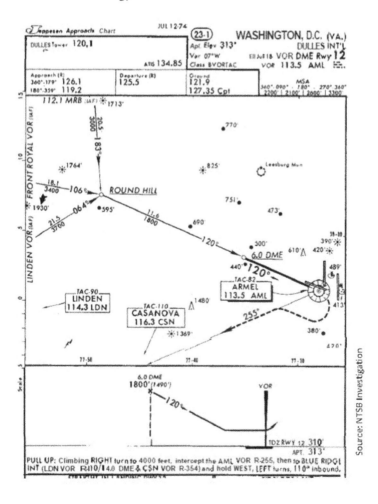

After United's 727 landing, the captain felt that something wasn't right about their approach. So the crew took the time to debrief their approach into Dulles. After examining the approach plate again, they realized they descended to the wrong altitude and were perilously low 25 miles from Dulles. The captain decided to write the report with the explanation on how they misinterpreted the clearance from approach control and how and why they descended early. Once the flight crew completed their FSAP report, it was submitted to United's **Event Review Committee (ERC).**

An ERC identifies human factors regarding the event (fatigue or communication), risk ranks the event, responds back to the reporter, and develops corrective action for the organization.

I've participated on hundreds of ERCs and established two BBS programs in oil and gas. The difference between a BBS program and the ASAP program is quite simple – a BBS program receives cards written solely to identify hazards. BBS programs won't receive cards based on unsafe acts because the reporter does not trust corporate leadership with an admission of making a mistake. An ASAP program has a dedicated team (ERC) to review cards and they do not blame the frontline workers for making honest mistakes. Most ERC cards are written like this, "I made a mistake…" (just like the card I wrote when I forgot to lower my flaps in Chapter 5). The ERC, well versed in human factors, understood that it was an honest mistake – that the near miss was not intentional, willful behavior.

United's informal investigation into the low altitude approach at Dulles identified a discrepancy in Dulles Approach clearances. United worked with the FAA to correct the poorly worded approach clearance from Dulles and United's Safety Department sent out a safety alert highlighting the event and lessons learned. But no formal, systematic corrective action was assigned from the learnings of this report.

One month later, December 1st, an American Airlines DC-9 was 44 miles to the west of Dulles International Airport. Just as with the United Airlines

727, Dulles Approach Control cleared American's DC-9 for the VOR DME Runway 12 approach without an altitude clearance. With the same poorly worded approach clearance, the DC-9 perilously descended to 1,800 feet. At 27 miles from Dulles (just seven miles from Mt. Weather), the captain of the DC-9 had a gut instinct that something was wrong. The captain called Dulles Approach Control and asked "What altitude should we be at?" The Dulles Approach Controller, utilizing their new radar, immediately told them to climb to 3,400 feet. The crew's gut instinct saved them and the DC-9 landed safely on Runway 12. The crew of TWA Flight 514 wouldn't be as fortunate.

Less than one hour later, TWA 514 descended into the Washington area destined for Capital Airport (now known as Reagan National). However, winds at Capital Airport were gusting greater than their 727's crosswind limitations. So, Captain Brock and his crew needed to update the weather at other local airports. The flight engineer dialed up weather information for Washington Dulles International Airport. There were low clouds, gusty winds, and rain mixed with occasional wet snow. But the wind blew straight down Runway 12 at Dulles and would allow a safe landing for the 727. The captain decided Dulles would be the divert airport for TWA 514.

At 10:50, Captain Brock checked in with Washington Center and requested to be vectored toward Washington Dulles Airport instead of Capital Airport. Washington Center assigned TWA 514 a new heading toward Dulles and requested they contact Dulles Approach. Dulles Approach told the crew to expect the VOR DME Runway 12 approach for landing. When flight crews divert an airplane from the originally filed destination, it can result in an initial high workload on the crew. High workloads caused by changing plans can be a recipe for human error.

Travelling at four miles a minute toward Dulles, the flight crew conducted a preliminary landing checklist that consisted of setting their altimeters to 29.74. Captain Brock reminded the crew of an intersection on the chart called Round Hill and the associated crossing altitude of 1,800 feet. First Officer Krescheck, an experienced co-pilot, determined the final approach speed for the aircraft would be 127 knots. They were all set to land at Dulles.

As the aircraft approached from the west, Dulles Approach Control gave instructions to descend to 7,000 feet. First Officer Krescheck turned off the autopilot and gently pushed forward on the control yoke. The 727 began its descent into the cold, cloudy Washington skies. At 45 miles west of Dulles, First Officer Krescheck began to level the aircraft at 7,000 feet when the Dulles Approach Controller cleared TWA 514 for the "VOR DME 12 approach." Captain Brock announced that the flight could continue its descent to 1,800 feet and that 1,800 feet "was the bottom." First Officer Krescheck stated, "Time to start down." He again pushed forward on the yoke and the 727 began its descent to 1,800 feet, 40 miles away from Runway 12.

Quietly behind the two pilots, the flight engineer stated, "We're out here quite a ways. I better turn the heat down." His comment was a reference to the temperature in the cabin and that the temperature gauge indicated that the cabin was hot in back. As the aircraft descended through 5,000 feet, the aircraft entered into continuous light turbulence.

As the 727 approached 1,800 feet, First Officer Krescheck pulled back on the yoke and leveled the aircraft off. He overshot his target altitude of 1,800 feet and leveled a little below 1,700 feet. Most of us have been on airplanes with turbulence – those subtle, jarring, uncontrolled airplane movements. The nervous flier may grab the armrests and perhaps squeeze out a prayer. For pilots, hand flying the aircraft can be task saturating. As First Officer Krescheck controlled the yoke, the turbulence made it difficult to maintain the assigned altitude. It took concentration. It channelized First Officer Krescheck's attention.

Autopilots are designed to decrease the pilots' workload in order to improve situational awareness and ultimately decision-making. Not only was TWA 514's altitude low, but their airspeed continued to fluctuate from the choppy turbulence. With the first officer's focus on the altitude and airspeed, he inadvertently dropped out a critical crosscheck – a comparison of where they were in perspective from Dulles to where they were on the approach plate (VOR DME Runway 12 approach). This failed crosscheck demonstrated the perilous impact channelized attention can have on a person and on a team.

TWA 514 was flying in and out of the base of the clouds when the captain stated, "We should break out." The black box would determine that First Officer Krescheck actually maintained 1,670 feet versus the minimum 1,800 feet. Legally, the flight crew was allowed a 300-foot buffer from 1,800 feet. However, this 130-foot error would be fatal.

As First Officer Krescheck fought the turbulence, he responded, "I hate the altitude jumping around." A few moments later, he added, "Gives you a headache after a while, watching the altitude jumping around like that." The captain, who was reviewing the approach plate for the VOR Runway 12 stated, "You know, according to this dumb sheet it says 3,400 feet to Round Hill intersection – our minimum altitude." The flight engineer asked the captain, "Where does it say that?" The captain responded by saying, "When approach control clears you, that means you can go to your…" He was interrupted by one of the crew members saying, "Initial approach altitude." The team unanimously agreed that 1,800 feet was the proper altitude and the 727 continued straight ahead toward Mt. Weather.

First Officer Krescheck was completely channelized on maintaining airspeed and altitude when Captain Brock commented, "You should see the ground outside in just a minute – hang in there!" The aircraft was skirting in and out of the cloud bases and the pockets of visual conditions would make it easier to see the runway. Seven seconds later, a warning horn sounded in the cockpit. It was recognized by Captain Brock who said, "Get some power on." In reality, the captain should have said, "Get the nose up!" Two seconds later, the horn sounded again and the 727 impacted the very top of Mount Weather approximately twenty miles from Dulles airport at an altitude of 1,670 feet.

Thirty seconds later, Dulles Approach Control said, "TWA 514, say your altitude." There was no answer.

Ninety-two crewmembers and passengers died on TWA Flight 514. But it wasn't a "one-out accident." It was an industry accident. The NTSB would discover that this crew's unsafe act had a history with almost all the air carriers flying into Dulles Airport. Other pilots had learned through tribal knowledge from the event, but a system did not exist that would allow the industry to learn from unsafe acts (honest mistakes), at least not yet.

For the NTSB, the cockpit voice recorder identified this as an operational accident and that the flight crew knowingly descended to an unsafe altitude of 1,800 feet versus the correct altitude of 3,400 feet after being cleared for the approach. But, why?

The pilots of TWA 514 had information regarding the elevation of obstacles west of Round Hill intersection (see diagram page 158). The flight crew was not based out of Dulles and was not familiar with all the obstacles around the airport. But the cockpit voice recorder did pick up an important human factor element that influenced the accident. It occurred when the captain was questioning the crew – "When Approach Control clears you, that means you can go to your..." The captain was interrupted by one of the crewmembers who said, "Initial approach altitude." This interruption and completion of the captain's statement by someone else is a characteristic of **confirmation bias**. Confirmation bias was so impactful that the crew would not bring up the low altitude again, and the flight remained at 1,670 feet.

> Confirmation bias describes a situation where a person will ignore facts or information that does not conform to their preconceived mental model, and will assume as true any information that does conform to their beliefs (Nickerson 1998)

So what made the flight crew of TWA 514 believe that they were safe to descend to such a low altitude so far from their destination? With over three decades of flight experience, I would be extremely uncomfortable descending an aircraft that far out to 1,800 feet. The investigators decided to examine the words that the Dulles Approach Controller used.

Commercial pilots are trained to understand that an approach clearance will also include an altitude assignment in a radar environment. But the controller issued a non-standard clearance on that fateful day. Dulles Approach stated, "TWA 514 cleared for the VOR DME approach." According to FAA standards, the Dulles Approach Controller should have stated, "TWA 514, descend and maintain 3,400 feet. When established on VOR DME 12 final segment, you are cleared for the approach."

Approach clearances are tightly defined and understood by both parties. The FAA handbook highlights that any radio call that effects a change in the responsibility for providing terrain clearance must be communicated and clearly understood by both pilots and controllers. This

> 50% of airline accidents have miscommunication between crews as a contributing cause. (Flight Safety Foundation 1990).

responsibility can never be **assumed.** No doubt, Captain Brock incorrectly assumed that Dulles Approach was watching their altitude. But Dulles Approach Control was not. It quickly became evident to the NTSB investigators that the lack of standardized communication played a key role for the fatal ending of TWA Flight 514.

The importance of standardized communication between work parties that eliminates assumptions in critical work cannot be over emphasized. For oil and gas, this was the case of Piper Alpha in 1988, where one shift failed to effectively communicate the status of the Lock Out/Tag Out of their high-pressure gas system to the on-coming shift. This miscommunication put in place the activation of a blocked natural gas line that lead to an explosion. Piper Alpha became the largest fatal accident in the North Sea killing 166 workers.

But soon the NTSB's investigators discovered multiple identical near misses with Mount Weather based on nonstandard communication from the Dulles Approach Controllers. A trend had been recorded but the weak signals of the impending accident were never heard at the corporate office. Hauntingly, the same miscommunication between Approach Control and another aircraft occurred again just **six** hours after TWA 514's accident.

In the end, the NTSB investigation determined that the probable cause was the crew's decision to descend to 1,800 feet versus 3,400 feet for the assigned approach segment. The crew's decision to descend was a lack of clarity in air traffic control procedures that led to a misunderstanding on the part of the pilots **and** of the controllers.

Once the causes and contributing causes were determined through the investigation, it was time to write the preventive corrective actions. The NTSB addressed the poor approach clearance delivered by Dulles Approach with the first three corrective actions in their report. In fact, these three corrective actions still keep us safe today.

But the fourth corrective action is pivotal for the airline industry. With the NTSB discovering the near miss report from United's FSAP, the NTSB team needed to find a solution to make learning systematic for an organization and for the entire industry. The investigators wrote the fourth corrective action to ensure learnings from the 88% of unsafe acts would be heard by corporate. It stated, "The FAA will establish an incident reporting system which is intended to identify unsafe operating conditions or unsafe acts in order to correct them before an accident occurs." This corrective action was the formal industry step of what is now called the Aviation Safety Action Program or ASAP.

Officially, ASAP is a formal (regulated), non-liability reporting system whereby an employee can tell his company, "I made a mistake and here's why." By fully revealing all of the causal factors and contributors to a mistake written by the "reporter," ASAP establishes that the value of knowledge from the frontline is critical in adjusting the safety culture. Here is how ASAP works.

Once a report is written, it is electronically submitted into the ASAP program. Next, the report goes to the ERC (the committee of analysts that has oversight of the ASAP program) who determines if the unsafe act was a deliberate action (criminal, substance abuse, reckless non-compliance, sabotage) by the individual that committed the act (known as the reporter). Unlike BBS programs, the ERC is staffed by corporate empowered decision makers – personnel such as safety, training, operations, union leaders, and the regulator. That's right. The regulator sits on the committee and has the final say on whether the report is accepted into the program or not. But all the members of the ERC share a rich understanding of human factors and that the human is not to blame. Instead, the report is an opportunity **to learn** why the human erred.

If the unsafe act is determined to be a willful, intentional act, the report is rejected and the event is handled through official corporate channels. This establishes the line of acceptable and unacceptable behavior, hence the term **"Just" Culture**. If the unsafe act was not a willful intentional act, then the report is accepted into the program so that the reporter can receive protection.

A Just Culture is described as an atmosphere of trust in which people are encouraged, even rewarded, for providing essential safety-related information, but in which they are also clear about where the line must be drawn between acceptable and unacceptable behavior. (*Reason 1990*)

The ERC's goal is to resolve all unsafe acts or conditions rather than to take legal enforcement or company disciplinary action against the employee or contractor. The ERC values the knowledge gained from the event more than blaming the individual.

The process is quite simple: an event occurs, knowledge is produced, procedures are changed, lessons are communicated, and culture is adjusted. With a drive to affect change in organizational procedures and processes, the ERC risk-ranks the incident. If the risk is high or a trend of similar type events (like altitude busts or poor approach clearances from Dulles Approach) is discovered, then procedures are changed. This incident reporting approach delivers practical solutions for the frontline and creates buy-in. Once the procedures are adjusted, the ERC waits to see if the changes reduce risk.

How effective is ASAP? US Airways had an altitude problem. During the course of a year, US Airways pilots had received 93 violations for flying to the wrong assigned altitude (known as an altitude bust). A violation meant that the FAA was aware of the mistake and issued a citation against the crew's certificates. But in this case, enough was enough. Ninety-three violations indicated a high risk to the corporation and it was time to find why it was happening and a means to prevent it. So, US Airways and the Air Line Pilots Association (ALPA) expanded the scope of reporting. Instead of reporting only because you committed a violation, the program asked every pilot to submit a report even if they caught the mistake and didn't end up at the wrong altitude. The program requested flight crews' near miss reports – Heinrich's 300 near misses. US Airways Safety Department needed to determine the "why" from all unsafe acts. They needed to understand in order to produce a corrective action that would reduce or eliminate this risk.

To collect these unsafe acts from the pilot group, the program granted amnesty to all reporting pilots for all events. With trust established in the program, the results were astonishing. Over a one-year period, 11,653 near miss reports were collected! In other words, US Airways thought they had 93 events but in reality they had 11,653 events – all in one year. With all this rich data on unsafe acts, common root causes started to surface and US Airways and ALPA were able put in place a new procedure regarding the setting of the altitude for pilots. How successful was the program? The year after the implementation of the new altitude setting procedure, US Airways had only 1,151 reports of near misses and **zero** violations. That's a 90% reduction in unsafe acts and zero reportable incidents. The ASAP program not only identified a tremendous source of data but also helped develop a practical corrective action for the frontline employee. Furthermore, the ASAP program was able to measure whether the newly designed altitude setting procedure was responsible for a reduction in unsafe acts. ASAP became the health test of US Airways' safety system.

Personally, I participated on an ERC for a large U.S. airline for five years. This experience gave me the opportunity to review over 30,000 reports of pilots informing management about how they made a mistake, an unsafe act. I had 30,000 opportunities to adjust our safety system. The program's success was built on the frontline workers' trust that we would not blame them for their errors but instead, would use their insights to learn. Through forty years of evolution, the tragic crash of TWA 514 delivered a safety program that has transformed the safety culture. In fact, it is the key element that transformed a blaming culture to a Just Culture.

Blaming cultures are prevalent in many industries. They evolve because people are less willing to inform their organizations about their own errors and other safety problems or hazards. This lack of trust in their employees prevents management from being properly informed of the actual risks to the workers and to the system. Managers are then unable to make the right decisions to improve safety. However, a "no-blame" culture is neither feasible nor desirable.

ASAP has been able to balance the concerns between an amnesty program for all unsafe acts and unintentional human error. It's a program that puts accountability on the frontline worker to report and accountability for staff members on how the report is handled.

To handle the report properly, it is necessary for the members to understand and acknowledge that people at the sharp end are not usually the instigators of accidents. In order for organizations to learn from incidents, it is necessary to recognize that human error will never be eliminated – only moderated. In order to combat human errors, we must change the conditions under which humans work. The effectiveness of countermeasures depends on the willingness of individuals to report their errors. This willingness relies on an atmosphere of trust in which people are encouraged to provide essential safety-related information. High reliable organizations are exceptional because they learn from their errors and **depend** on receiving reports from the frontline about their failures. Failures spur innovation and improvement.

How effective could a Just Culture be in other industries? An explosion occurred at British Petroleum's (BP) Texas City Refinery on March 23,

2005, when a hydrocarbon vapor cloud was ignited and violently exploded at the Isomerization (ISOM) Process Unit. Fifteen workers were killed and more than 180 were injured. The refinery was severely damaged. At the time of the incident, the Texas City Refinery was the third largest in the United States with an input capacity of 437,000 barrels of oil per day. The investigation determined numerous causal factors to the fatal accident. Some of the key failures that set the explosion chain in motion included:

- A defective management of change process (which allowed the siting of contractor trailers too close to the ISOM Process Unit);
- Inadequate training of operators;
- Lack of competent supervision for start-up operations;
- Poor communications between individuals and departments;
- The use of outdated and ineffective work procedures that were often not followed;
- A blowdown drum that was of insufficient size;
- Lack of preventative maintenance on safety critical systems; and
- Inoperative alarms and level sensors in the ISOM Process.

If Texas City had an ASAP program, the above contributing causes would have been submitted months before the fatal accident. The ERC would have moved trailers farther away, inoperative alarms would have been repaired, and the insufficient blowdown drum would have been replaced. In essence, the frontline would have trusted management to make the necessary changes in order to improve safety.

This is not speculation. The above conditions are identical to the reports that I reviewed on a weekly basis written by frontline pilots. We read the reports, made changes to the operating system and generated trust with the frontline. In my opinion, Texas City would have had a plethora of reports on the above contributing causes prior to their accident. But what was missing was an understanding that the frontline would make honest mistakes and corporate didn't have the means to learn from them.

After the fatal explosion, the Chemical Safety Board (CSB) identified BP as having a "poor safety culture" – an obvious assessment from the investigation. But the label of "poor culture" does not provide corrective actions that will be preventative. Instead, the CSB needed to deliver a tool that improved culture; a tool that shifted a culture from blaming to learning about why the frontline errs. CSB should have mandated the implementation of the ASAP program.

It's not just the oil and gas industry that could benefit from a Just Culture. The medical industry could as well. The third leading cause of deaths in the U.S. is human error – up to 250,000 deaths per year (Macary 2005). The joint Commission (formerly JCAHO) recommends instituting an organization-wide program of transparency to shed light on all adverse events from unsafe acts such as:

- Two nurses select the wrong medication from the dispensing system. One dose reaches a patient, causing him to go into shock. The other mistake is caught at the bedside before causing harm.
- A nurse loses custody of an unlabeled specimen but chooses not to report the incident out of fear of discipline.
- An entire surgical team skips the pre-surgical timeout. (Griffith 2009)

For the airline industry, ASAP has become the proven program that identifies why and how doctors and nurses make mistakes. In fact, ASAP identifies Heinrich's 88% of unrecorded unsafe acts that healthcare needs in order to be preventative in human error, not the 12% that gets recorded. Reports that acknowledge that competent professionals develop unhealthy norms, errors represent predictable mistakes between humans and the system in which they work and individuals cannot be held accountable for system failings over which they have no control.

ASAP highlights to management how human error is inevitable in any system. It must be continually monitored and improved to accommodate these errors. And individuals are accountable for their actions – especially if they knowingly violate safety procedures or policies. But the single greatest impediment to error prevention is that corporate punishes their workers for making mistakes. Period.

The airlines have proven that the effectiveness of the learnings from ASAP can become contagious to other employee groups as well. In my experience, three other employee divisions adopted ASAP because of the pilot group success with it (dispatchers, mechanics, and flight attendants). Today, the airline industry has over 170 participating programs and an enviable mishap rate of zero. ASAP became the generative step in safety.

ASAP's sole objective is to learn as much as possible about why human error (a mistake) occurred and to devise corrections to reduce the likelihood of that error occurring again. ASAP fosters a spirit of cooperation and its success can be measured in a simple count of the same mistakes occurring in the future. ASAP is the engine for organizational learning.

References:

Aircraft Accident Report, Trans World Airlines, Inc. Boeing 727-23, N54328, Berryville, Virginia, December 1, 1974, NTSB.

FAA advisory circular on Aviation Safety Action Program, 11/15/02 AC No: 12-66B.

Griffith, K. S. 2009. "Column: The Growth of a Just Culture." *The Joint Commission Perspectives on Patient Safety* 9:12:8–9.

Investigation Report, Refinery Explosion and Fire, BP, Texas City, Texas, March 23, 2005.

Makary, Martin and Daniel, Michael. 2016. "Study suggests medical errors now third leading cause of death in the U.S." *Johns Hopkins Medicine* May 3, 2016 175.

Nickerson, Raymond S. 1998. "Confirmation Bias: A Ubiquitous Phenomenon in Many Guises" *Review of General Psychology* 2(2), 175-220.

8

Organizational Learning

*"Those who cannot remember the past are
condemned to repeat it."*
Jorge Santayana

Jorge Santayana was a Spanish philosopher who correctly identified why CEOs and safety professionals are condemned to see the same accident occurring again and again within their safety system. There's no permanent memory of the lessons learned. Most corporations lack an effective strategic learning process. No doubt, corporate will send out a sterile safety alert warning others about the event in order to prevent similar incidents. But these alerts rarely change behavior of frontline personnel. In order to have an impact on corporate's management system, the lesson learned from an accident needs to be cemented into frontline step-by-step procedures. Human factors has taught us that we are not perfect and that those lessons learned belong at the strategic level, not the tactical. Only when your CEO switches from a horizontal learning system of safety alerts to a vertical system of corporate learning, will the next step change in safety occur.

Organizational or vertical learning is the foundation, the bedrock, of a high reliable organization. To establish

Organizational or vertical learning is the process of creating, retaining, and transferring knowledge within an organization and modifying the behavior of the workforce to reflect new knowledge and insights. (Harvard Business Review 1993)

a vertical learning system, two elements are required. First, leadership must promote the importance of learning, including providing appropriate funding. Secondly, the corporation must adopt a learning process that creates, retains, transfers, and modifies frontline worker behavior. Long-term corporate success depends on departing from the traditional horizontal learning style (word of mouth through safety alerts or tribal knowledge) throughout the organization and develop a learning system, a process that moves vertically as well.

It is a fact that all organizations, over time, gain lessons learned. It is what the organization does with those lessons that make it stand out. It is what makes the organization pull ahead of their competitors in the hyper-competitive world in which they operate. Successful vertical learning corporations have the ability to shape the behavior of the workforce and raise the bar on operational performance. And there's one American company that does it better than anyone else. It's Boeing.

William Boeing left a legacy for innovation driven by a desire for excellence by establishing a systematic corporate vertical learning system. In the early 1970s, Boeing was leading the industry in ingenuity and engineering but was concerned with "What's next?" So, Boeing studied the successes and failures of their previous three airplane designs (727,737 and 747), manufacturing processes, and launches of their aircraft. Corporate leadership didn't want to rely upon their past successes and therefore, created a team called "Project Homework." The focus of Project Homework was to prevent repetition of past failures and to develop the next generation aircraft with those lessons embedded into their work processes. Armed with the CEO's vision and dedicated resources (money and personnel), Project Homework developed hundreds of lessons learned over a three-year period. In the end, the team stumbled into a startling discovery. Project Homework didn't recommend an aircraft to corporate headquarters. Instead they recommended two: the 767 *and* the 757.

These two aircraft couldn't be more different. The 767 is designed to fly from the U.S. to Europe. It is powered by two engines with a combined thrust of 100,000 pounds and carries up to 350 people. The 757 is designed to fly transcontinental routes or short-haul domestic flights. It is powered by two engines with a combined thrust of 76,000 pounds and carries up to 220 people. The missions, size, and power of these two aircraft require completely different systems. However, Project Homework directed Boeing to develop two aircraft simultaneously that contained the same flight management systems, same engineering designs to capture fuel efficiency, and the standardization of a two-person cockpit (versus three). In the end, Boeing's customers were richly rewarded. Customers received two completely different mission capable aircraft that could be flown by the same pilot. All of this was accomplished from a focus on lessons learned and procedural standardization. Project Homework's delivery of the 757 and 767 kept Boeing on top of the industry for its creativity and proved the value of gathering the learnings from past decisions. Boeing set the corporate standard for vertical organizational learning and was rewarded for it.

With decades of vertical organizational learning behind them, Boeing has evolved their organizational learning cycle (knowledge management) to the following model:

- Improve access to the expert;
- Preserve key knowledge;
- Leverage knowledge to enhance performance; and
- Institutionalize the Boeing knowledge network. *(Boeing et. al.)*

The first step in Boeing's corporate process identifies where the majority of the learning for the organization occurs – improved access to the expert. The importance of the first step cannot be overlooked.

Following the successful launch of the 757 and 767, Boeing again found itself in the position to be the first in the industry to develop the next generation aircraft. In the early 1990s, armed with corporate leadership that fully supported vertical organizational learning, the company enhanced the first step of their corporate learning model. They included United Airlines captains into the design, build, and launch phases of a new aircraft that would eventually be called the 777. The conceptual design of the 777 started in 1990 and in just five years United Airlines took delivery of the first aircraft – an incredible feat. Furthermore, the first delivered aircraft was virtually defect-free upon acceptance, another industry first. Today, the 777 is the safest airplane on record and the most successful selling wide-body aircraft ever made. With a laser focus that utilized the expert (the airline captain), Boeing raised the prevention of human error to the next level. They listened to the pilot's perspective – the end user – and delivered an aircraft with a safety record second to none.

Boeing's strategic commitment to vertical organizational learning has seen the company become the leader in multiple industries (commercial aircraft, space, military hardware) and the dependence on learning has grown Boeing's revenue to over $96 billion and over 160,000 employees (2015). Today, Boeing has established learning curves for every workstation in its assembly plant – workstations that assist in monitoring productivity, determining workflows (step-by-step procedures), and setting profit margins for new airplanes. Boeing is an established industry leader because it has a vertical learning system that prevents it from making the same mistake twice.

Regardless of the industry, corporate leadership owes new employees step-by-step procedures based on lessons learned. Several years ago, I was a simulator instructor on the Airbus 319 and 320. My job responsibility was to teach step-by-step procedures in full flight visual simulators. Tightly written, manicured procedures, along with virtual flight simulators, assisted the airlines to replicate efficiencies and safety while flying the paying public around the world. Combined, they deliver a predictable outcome for each and every flight. In fact, the last seventeen years have been fatality-free in the United States because of this vertical learning system. But other industries haven't established a vertical learning system. Instead, corporate continues to add layer upon layer of policy statements, safety alerts, and the reliance of frontline leadership to control or prevent mistakes from recurring. This lack of organizational learning will fail corporate leadership.

Ultra-Deepwater, semi-submersible drill ships (rigs) are dynamically positioned and operate in waters up to 8,000 feet (2,400 meters) deep. Over 150 personnel on board drill wells to a maximum depth of 30,000 feet (9,100 meters). Each well is the culmination of solving some of the most difficult engineering problems of the 21st century. One of the greatest threats to a drilling team is that the reservoir into which they drill is under significant pressure. Therefore, drill crews must maintain greater pressure on the fluid column within the wellbore in order to prevent the reservoir's oil and gas from racing toward the surface. This philosophy is called well control. The crew's understanding of this pressure relationship is critical to the safety of the crew and drillship. When the pressure is greater from the reservoir than the hydrostatic column of fluid, a blowout can occur.

On December 23, 2009, the Sedco 711, an ultra-deep water semi-submersible ship, was performing a test on the recent oil/gas well that it had completed in the North Sea. The negative pressure test was to determine if the mechanical barrier, also known as cement, was sufficiently sealed. Unnoticed by the crew, the test failed and the cement failed to maintain the pressures deep down in the reservoir. Twenty minutes later, the Sedco 711 had water, mud, high-pressure natural gas, and broken drill pipe shooting out of the rotary table, covering the entire rig. The only reason the rig didn't catch fire was that the gas cloud did not find an ignition source. With mud and gas hissing from the rotary table, the crew immediately realized they had a severe well control event (a blowout) and activated the blowout preventer. Sedco 711's blowout preventer closed the well and put an end to this potentially fatal accident.

The investigation into this incident identified the failure of the underbalanced or negative inflow test. But the crew should have identified the failed test while performing the procedure, not after the well blew out. So, why did the crew not detect the well kick? The investigators discovered that the mud returns were being routed to reserve pits that prevented the crew from monitoring the returns on the active pit system (this routing was against company policy). This bad practice hid the real condition of the well as it raced toward the surface. Other well control parameters were not interpreted as loss of well control based on the crew's false faith in the "successful" well barrier test (plan continuation bias). As the high-pressure gas raced toward the drill ship, the drill crew rationalized that the well barrier was holding (when in fact, it had failed). Transocean's (owner of Sedco 711) investigation into this event identified three causes of the well blowout:

- Failure of the tested downhole barrier;
- Failure of the crew to monitor and identify the influx; and
- Failure to close in the well prior to the influx reaching the BOP.

These were all important lessons from which other frontline workers should learn. Furthermore, these learnings should have been broken down into step-by-step procedures and inserted into a vertical learning system in order to prevent recurrence. But it was handled differently.

Transocean did send out a safety alert (horizontal learning) to inform other drill ships of their recommendations:

- Increase communication of Standing Instructions to the Driller (SID) with clear roles, accountability, and responsibilities (left open for interpretation);
- Develop and use written work instructions for well control operations that include guidance information on overbalance and underbalance operations and on conducting inflow tests (no standardization); and
- Review of the Transocean (contractor) and Shell (operator) bridging document to clarify accountabilities and standardize the well control process into defined phases that identify when decision making requires management or technical onshore support (ambiguous).

The above recommendations look good on paper but are a recipe for disaster.

Fast-forward three months to April 20, 2010. The Transocean's Deepwater Horizon had correctly performed a positive inflow test on the Macondo Well (same procedure as Sedco 711) and was conducting an underbalanced or negative inflow test. But the negative inflow test failed and the well was flowing toward the ship (just as with Sedco 711). In the driller's shack, the crew did not detect the well kick (underbalanced condition) in part, because the mud returns were being routed against company policy and prevented the crew from monitoring the returns on the active pit system. Well control parameters located on instruments were not interpreted as indicators of loss of well control based on the crew's false faith in the successful well barrier test. The parameters were clearly indicating that mud was racing toward the surface but the drill crew was convinced it was not. It was the exact same scenario on board the Sedco 711, just three months earlier.

The blowout on the Deepwater Horizon hit the rig floor with significant force spewing oil, gas, water, and mud over the entire rig. However, unlike the Sedco 711, the natural gas cloud found a spark and ignited. After the explosion, the crew attempted to shut in the well utilizing the BOP (blowout preventer); however, the BOP did not function properly and the rig burned. The fire could not be extinguished and two days later, Deepwater Horizon sank. The explosion killed eleven crewmen and injured seventeen. The Macondo Well would continue to gush a total of 130 million gallons of oil into the Gulf of Mexico for the next 87 days at a cost of over 60 billion dollars.

The U.S. Chemical Safety Board's investigation revealed that the advisory or safety alert on the loss of well control on Sedco 711 never made it to the Deepwater Horizon crew. The government investigation highlighted a laissez-faire approach regarding the passing on of lessons learned from the Sedco 711 incident to other offshore facilities. Transocean's General Manager of North America, who was responsible for forwarding the information to other Gulf of Mexico drilling rigs, stated that the email containing the advisory came in while he was on vacation and that he never saw it. Another person covered the general manager's duties while he was on vacation, but upon review of both email accounts, neither person forwarded the advisory to employees working in the Gulf of Mexico. Although the advisory was posted on Transocean's internal electronic document system, employees had to subscribe for notifications of newly added documents. This "fire and forget" PowerPoint methodology of passing on lessons learned will not change frontline behavior. Horizontal learning is ineffective and unreliable.

Instead, the learnings of Sedco 711 needed to be embedded into a vertical learning system – a vertical learning system that translates the recommendations into detailed step-by-step procedures (or checklists) instead of being left for the field to loosely interpret on their own. Once standardized, corporate must receive acknowledgement that the frontline workers have received, understood, and implemented the changes. Corporate quality will then audit the field to the changes and the organization becomes safer – changing frontline worker's behavior.

I have spent decades on the corporate safety side, one that standardizes learnings from incidents into step-by-step procedures that changed how I flew airplanes. But American Airlines Flight 587 delivered a procedural change to all Airbus pilot's step-by-step procedures – changes that impacted my life.

With U.S. airlines flying over 895 million passengers on 9.5 million flights in 2016 (Bureau of Transportation Statistics), loss of control in flight is recognized as one of the top risks to the aviation industry. LOC (loss of control) accidents are typically caused by an aircraft wake or severe weather events.

As a passenger, wake turbulence feels like a sudden roll or jolt that grabs your attention but then quickly eases as the aircraft exits the encounter. It's like hitting a speed bump in your neighborhood while driving too fast. But for the pilot, it can develop into an uncommanded roll that, in extreme cases, can be beyond the absolute power of the flying controls or the prevailing response of the flight crew to counteract. There are several major, high profile accidents that resulted in lost lives due to wake turbulence from aircraft taking off immediately following another aircraft. In fact, when the Boeing 757 was first introduced, it was initially designated with an unsafe separation distance. This minimum separation between a 757 and another aircraft was subsequently increased after the president of the In-N-Out Burger restaurant chain was killed in a small aircraft that followed a Boeing 757 into Orange County Airport. However, pilots are not the only ones in charge of safe separation of aircraft. Air traffic controllers share responsibility for assuring that arriving and departing aircraft avoid the previous aircraft's wake turbulence. The FAA Air Traffic Control Handbook indicates that the separation for a heavy airplane behind another heavy airplane is two minutes or four nautical miles. Both pilots and controllers strictly adhere to these minimums.

Not only is there a threat of wake turbulence at takeoff or landing, but the threat can also occur as a cross-track encounter at cruise altitude. These encounters lead to one or two sharp 'jolts' as the vortices of the aircraft above are crossed. In either case, injuries to unsecured passengers or crews can occur.

I had never encountered significant wake turbulence at altitude until I entered the commercial airline industry. It was nighttime and I was a first officer on the 727. It was a clear, beautiful, and turbulent free night and we watched an aircraft pass overhead with the acceptable 1,000 foot of clearance. Then, we suddenly hit that speed bump. Hard. I grabbed the controls and waited to see how the encounter would develop. Luckily, two seconds later we were in smooth air again. It taught me to be proactive with the seat belt sign in anticipation of another aircraft's wake, not after.

So what is wake turbulence? Wake turbulence is the potentially hazardous turbulence in the wake of an aircraft that is caused by wing tip vortices. This type of turbulence can be significant because wing tip vortices decay slowly and can produce a significant rotational influence on an aircraft encountering them for several minutes after they have been generated.

As a pilot, it is important to understand that the strength of the vortex is governed by the weight, speed, and shape of the wing of the generating aircraft.

Vortices usually persist for one-to-three minutes depending on wind conditions.

Once formed, vortices descend until they decay (or reach the ground). (SKYbrary)

This flying phenomenon has been studied by NASA for years. The worst-case scenario for an encounter with hazardous wake vortex turbulence is greatest when your aircraft follows the same departure track immediately after a heavier aircraft departs from a runway. Therefore, wake turbulence is mostly encountered close to the ground in the vicinity of airports where aircraft are on departure from particular runways at high frequencies. This was the environment in which American Airlines Flight 587 departed from JFK.

On November 12, 2001, New York's JFK Tower cleared a JAL Boeing 747 for takeoff, destined for Tokyo, Japan. The Boeing 747 is one of the heaviest aircraft ever to fly. It can weigh over 900,000 pounds on departure. Right after rotating, all aircraft will produce wing tip vortices below and behind the aircraft path and JAL 747 will create some of the strongest wing tip vortices of any type of aircraft. With takeoff clearance from the tower, the JAL 747 began the takeoff roll and lifted off 7,000 feet down the runway. As the JAL 747 began rolling down the runway, JFK Tower cleared American Airlines Flight 587 into position onto the same runway. The American Airlines' captain steered the large Airbus 300 into position and set the parking brake. He handed control of the aircraft over to the first officer. The first officer placed his hands on the throttles and waited for takeoff clearance from tower. Moments later, JFK Tower cleared AA 587 for takeoff.

A few seconds after the captain acknowledged the takeoff clearance, the first officer asked the captain, "Are you happy with our separation?" The captain replied, "We'll be all right once we get rolling. The JAL 747 is supposed to be at least five miles away by the time we're airborne; that's the idea." The first officer said, "So you're happy." The first officer released the parking brake and moved the throttles forward. AA 587 engines roared to life one minute and 40 seconds after the Japan Air Lines 747 took off. Even though AA 587 rolled less than two minutes from the JAL 747, the two aircraft were separated at all times by at least 4.3 nm horizontally and 3,800 feet vertically (a legal separation).

At 160 miles per hour, rotation speed, the Airbus first officer smoothly pulled back on the yoke and the large aircraft lifted off the runway headed for the Dominican Republic. With a positive rate of climb, the captain raised the landing gear. Moments later, the JFK Tower controller instructed the pilots of Flight 587 to "turn left, fly the bridge departure, and contact the New York departure controller." About five seconds later, the captain acknowledged this instruction and the first officer flew the assigned route. Thirty seconds later, the captain made initial contact with the departure controller, "AA 587 is passing 1,300 feet and climbing to 5,000 feet." The departure controller instructed Flight 587 to climb to and maintain 13,000 feet and the captain acknowledged the new altitude. The captain read and completed the "After Takeoff Checklist," verifying that the aircraft was clean and that it was safe for the first officer to accelerate their Airbus to 250 knots.

American Airlines Flight 587 was climbing through 1,700 feet with its wings approximately level when the airplane experienced its first encounter with wake turbulence from the JAL 747. At the controls, the first officer felt this first wake turbulence encounter and responded by moving the control column (the yoke) and rudder pedals to counter the turbulence thus keeping the aircraft under control.

Since wake turbulence is a designated high-risk or high-hazard occurrence, all major airlines have training programs that address recovery techniques when pilots encounter it. Five years prior to Flight 587, American Airlines along with Airbus, developed their upset training program from the review of worldwide accidents from 1987 to 1996. But American Airlines training was conducted in the simulator under clear air turbulence conditions and not specifically tied to wake turbulence from another aircraft. Furthermore, use of the rudder by the pilot to counter the turbulence was advocated in maintaining control of the aircraft, not banned. In other words, the pilots of AA 587 were trained at altitude to recover from turbulence and to use rudder when needed to help maintain control of the aircraft.

The captain of Flight 587 stated, "Little wake turbulence, huh?" to which the first officer replied, "Yeah." Several seconds later, the air began to smooth out and the aircraft accelerated toward 250 knots. As the aircraft achieved 250 knots, the Airbus flew into a second wake turbulence encounter from the JAL 747. This time, the first officer countered the turbulence with more aggressive bank angles, control wheel, and exaggerated rudder movements than the first encounter. The first officer stated, in a strained voice, "max power." Moments later, the captain questioned him, "You all right?" The first officer quickly replied, "Yeah, I'm fine." The aircraft continued to be pushed by the turbulence and one second later, the captain stated, "Hang onto it. Hang onto it." Once again in a strained voice, the first officer stated, "Let's go for power please." Unbeknownst to the crew, a large crack occurred in the vertical stabilizer located on the tail of the aircraft during the second encounter. The first officer again pushed hard on the rudder pedal to the left and then suddenly reversed or cycled the rudder to the right. This fifth severe "rudder reversal" fractured the vertical stabilizer on the tail of the aircraft. As the aircraft began to uncontrollably slip sideways, the first officer said, "Holy [expletive]." The captain stated, "What the hell are we into. We're stuck in it." The last words from the captain were, "Get out of it. Get out of it."

There were 265 fatalities (all 260 on board and 5 on the ground). Tragically, American Airlines Flight 587 became the second deadliest aviation accident in U.S. history.

The digital flight recorder was the key on which the NTSB focused during their investigation. After first review, the team of investigators narrowed the search for the cause of the accident to the wake turbulence encounter. Immediately after the onset of Flight 587's second wake turbulence encounter (about seven seconds before the vertical stabilizer separation), the flight data recorder recorded a series of five large cyclic movements of the rudder on the vertical stabilizer.

The NTSB ran tests on the autopilot and rudder system and concluded that the only way to move the rudder in a manner that matched Flight 587's FDR (Flight Data Recorder) trace was for the pilot to depress the rudder pedals. Therefore, the investigators concluded that Flight 587's cyclic rudder motions after the second wake turbulence encounter were the result of the first officer's significant rudder pedal inputs.

The investigators noted that during the time that the first officer was making the five cyclic rudder pedal inputs, the captain began to question him (at 0915:55 he asked, "You all right?") and coached him (at 0915:56 he said, "Hang on to it."). However, the captain did not intervene or take control of the airplane, which would have been within his authority as captain. The NTSB report commented, "It appears that the captain believed that the wake was causing the airplane motion, even after the vertical stabilizer had separated from the airplane (saying, "Get out of it. Get out of it."). Furthermore, it would have been difficult for the captain to observe the first officer's rudder pedal inputs. Accordingly, given the captain's limited knowledge of the circumstances and the short duration of the accident sequence, the captain's response to the situation was understandable. Therefore, it would've been difficult, if not impossible, for the captain to understand why the airplane was responding like it was. The captain didn't have much of a role in this particular accident.

The NTSB's investigation dug into American Airlines wake turbulence recovery training. American's recovery procedure recommended the use of the rudders in order to counter the upset attitude of the aircraft, which is acceptable at slow airspeeds. But AA 587 was fast – 250 knots fast. Therefore, the NTSB determined that American Airline pilots (and the industry) had little exposure to the effect of large rudder pedal inputs in normal flight (250 knots or greater). Furthermore, within the training course, pilots were not well-trained regarding the airplane's reduction in rudder pedal travel with increasing airspeed (the faster the aircraft is going, the less rudder deflection is required for the same effect). NTSB determined training played a role within the accident sequence.

In the end, the NTSB determined that the probable cause of this accident was the in-flight separation of the vertical stabilizer as a result of the loads beyond ultimate design that were created by the first officer's unnecessary and excessive rudder pedal inputs. The investigators also determined that contributing to the accident were elements of the American Airlines upset recovery program.

But what made this accident "personal" for me was a bulletin – a bulletin that Airbus distributed to all companies that flew Airbuses.

Here's the solution from Airbus's bulletin. The first recommended change to the corporate operating procedure was to include this **CAUTION** for the corporate's Airbus manual:

> *Sudden commanded full, or nearly full, opposite rudder movement against a sideslip can generate loads that exceed the limit loads and possibly the ultimate loads and can result in structural failure.*

The second recommendation for addition into the operating procedures was:

> *Whatever the airborne flight condition may be, aggressive, full or nearly full, opposite rudder inputs must not be applied. Such inputs can lead to loads higher than the limit, or possibly the ultimate loads and can result in structural damage or failure. The rudder travel limiter system is not designed to prevent structural damage or failure in the event of such rudder system inputs. Rudder reversals must never be incorporated into an airline policy.*

In 2001, I was an Airbus pilot for a major U.S. airline. After this accident, an initial safety alert was sent to the frontline personnel reminding us of the lessons learned – horizontal learning. But my airline company was busy determining how to incorporate these unfortunate learnings into their long-term memory – vertical learning. The only effective way to change frontline behavior was to transfer these lessons into standardized step-by-step procedures. Then train their crews on the upset recovery procedures in order to get an expected outcome (the definition of a procedure). The adjusted simulator course highlighted the structural effects of full rudder movement on the tail, discussed the effects of a rudder reversal at high airspeeds, and that maximum rudder deflection can be obtained with comparatively little or light pedal forces.

After discussing these limitations in the brief, we executed the new procedure – without the use of rudder in a full visual flight simulator. The simulator is extremely effective at changing frontline behavior (key to learning). Cognitive scientists have observed, "It is very difficult to become knowledgeable in a passive way. Actively experiencing something is considerably more valuable than having it described to you." This new procedure became embedded into my System 1 processor.

In Chapter 1, I shared a personal flight incident in which our aircraft was impacted by severe turbulence. During our severe upset event, my feet firmly remained on the floor during my recovery maneuver. But not because of a safety alert from six years earlier, but from the addition of the lessons from AA 587 into our flight manuals along with a training curriculum. I was systematically trained on these lessons learned in order for my company to get the predictable response from this high-risk event. Our severe turbulent event became a "non-event" because of the corporate learning system in place - not because of the skill set of the pilots flying that day. It was a system success story and the best organizational learning success story that I know.

But the importance of vertical learning cannot be over-emphasized. Jack Welch, the former CEO of GE said, "An organization's ability to learn, and translate that learning into action rapidly, is the ultimate competitive advantage." Jack Welch valued learning in order to stimulate change and called it "boundarylessness" which became a cornerstone and successful corporate strategy for GE. It's not just Jack Welch who knows what separates the leader from the pack. Peter Senge, a noted MIT scientist and author of the book, *"The Fifth Discipline: The Art and Practice of the Learning Organization"* states that "the concept of a learning organization is increasingly relevant given the increasing complexity and uncertainty of the organizational environment." He further believes, "The rate at which organizations learn may become the only sustainable source of competitive advantage." To become the leader in your industry you must transform your organization into a vertical learning organization.

But what holds organizations back from this competitive advantage is the inability to acquire learnings from the frontline. But the airlines have an edge in this area compared to all other industries. It's ASAP. ASAP opened a vault of key opportunities to learn from. Learnings which weren't driven by investigations but instead from the frontline's trust on reporting their mistakes. But ASAP wasn't just for safety. When fuel unexpectedly accelerated to $90 a barrel, our ASAP group received thousands of reports on how to save fuel. Reports that highlighted the cost of carrying the weight of the magazine Skymall to the amount of revenue that was received (Skymall filed Chapter 11). ASAP became the greatest source for learning at the corporate level. Over the last decade, hospitals, energy companies, manufacturing and other industries have observed the ERC in an attempt to initiate ASAP into their corporate learning system.

ASAP is the crown jewel for organizational learning, but there's one other frontline tool that can help as well. It's called the debrief. As a young fighter pilot in a U.S. Marine Corps squadron, I was raised in an environment of constant professional criticism based on my performance. With detailed step by step procedures providing the foundation on how we deviated, we would always find a way to improve execution. And this process drove success. Lots of corporations have begun the journey of instilling the debrief into the corporate learning culture. Below is a simple template that is often found within these corporations.

- What did we set out to do?
- What actually happened?
- Why did it happen?
- What do we do next time?

But having a template doesn't deliver effective debriefings. There are three barriers that prevent corporations from simply adopting this successful frontline tool and begin winning. First, we continue to blame our frontline workers for their mistakes. Instead, error needs to be embraced, celebrated as an opportunity to learn, and not used to shame others. Debriefing our minor mistakes creates team unity and an atmosphere of trust. Secondly, cognitive dissonance gets in our way. Cognitive dissonance is a term Festinger (1962) defined that relates to the inner tension that we feel when we believe our work is being challenged – that we are wrong. It comes from the internal belief that we know we are smart, that we don't make mistakes. When we feel that inner tension swell up inside, we deploy tactics like self-justification or we reframe the event (the equipment failed not me) rather than admit we erred. Cognitive dissonance prevents the debrief from getting to the facts of the event. Thirdly, you must have step-by-step procedures. Corporate step-by-step procedures provide the single source document that tells the worker exactly how the work should be performed. Without standards, there is no ability for one person's work to be more correct than another's.

The template isn't key, it's how you debrief. The leader must use a crew-centered approach that draws upon the professional experience and motivation to perform well and to learn. Adults learn and remember more when they actively participate and make their own analysis rather than being passive to someone else's analysis. Active participation drives a deeper review and allows the team to draw upon the detail in order to capture lessons learned. Once again, the anchor that delivers detail is the corporate step-by-step procedures. Furthermore, referencing corporate procedures will create the necessary "buy-in" from those that follow procedures.

If corporate leaders would adopt a culture that recognizes that we all make errors and embrace learning from our mistakes, then progress would quickly ensue.

The medical industry hasn't been very successful at adopting the debrief culture. The FDA published a paper highlighting the frequency of the same miss-prescribed medical error in the U.S. It turns out this one repeated error injured 1.3 million patients each year in the U.S. – a missed opportunity to learn for sure.

I have learned many times during a productive debrief. But what about the organization? In the Marine Corps, combat lessons learned are quickly sent vertically up the chain of command for standardization and approval. Standards are rewritten, Marines are notified of the changes, training is updated, and frontline behavior is successfully changed. For an organization to evolve into a high reliable organization, a standardization department is a must. In fact, the most successful story of implementing a standardization department is the United States Navy.

In 1954, the U.S. Navy and Marine Corps had a safety problem. The accident rate was 55 major accidents per thousand flight hours. This translated to 776 aircraft and 535 aviators lost in just one year! The root of the issue was the pilots' flying habits from slow piston airplanes were unsafe in the high-speed world of jets. The U.S. Navy's solution was to standardize the methodology for every new pilot to be exposed to the best and safest procedure on how to fly these modern high-speed jets. Here's how they institutionalized standardization into a large organization that was already operating at full speed ahead.

Frontline workers (subject matter experts) would write down their current best practices in a step-by-step manner. Once drafted, the experts invited every pilot and user to recommend changes and modifications to them. All inputs were reviewed by corporate and updated when applicable. The operating manual would be formalized. When a pilot wanted to change a procedure he would submit a change notice. Once approved by corporate, this change notice would go back to the squadrons. Manuals would change, pilots were notified, and they began flying their aircraft to the new standard. When these new formal operating standards (step-by-step procedures) were sent to the squadrons, the pilots were often heard commenting, "It's about time!" Pilots no longer had to fly airplanes according to their boss's experience or demands. Shortcuts were removed in operations and an immediate impact on reliability and safety was achieved. The mishap rate drastically dropped and there were significant improvements in operational readiness. The U.S. Navy learned that frontline work procedures need to be uniformly framed when distributed in order to reduce misinterpretations by the frontline workers. Just five years later, standardization was institutionalized at the top level of the Navy and it received the official name of NATOPS (Naval Aviation Training and Operations Procedures Standardization). Not only did NATOPS teach experienced pilots how to fly safely but it became the competency tool for new fighter pilots as well. Standardization was the key strategic principle that significantly lowered the U. S. Navy and Marine accident rate – a measurable step change in safety and operations for sure.

Any organization striving to be a high reliable organization can't just issue procedures and expect overnight success. Training to procedures is not a luxury; it is a competitive and strategic necessity. In today's ultra-competitive and constantly changing landscape, training is not just a matter of survival; it is what separates the best from the rest.

The corporate winners of the 21st century will be the companies that install a vertical learning system – a vertical learning system that can successfully create, retain, transfer, and train (which modifies behavior) to reflect new knowledge and insights on how the frontline conducts work. That organization will out-maneuver its competitors and sit alone at the top.

References

Airbus Industrie A300-605R N14053. 2001. "In-Flight Separation of Vertical Stabilizer, American Airlines Flight 587 Belle Harbor, New York." *NTSB*. November 12, 2001.

Airbus 310 / A300-600. 2002. "Use of Rudder on transport category airplanes." FCOM Bulletin No 15/1, Date: March 2002.

Ashkenas, Ron. 2015. "Jack Welch's Approach to Breaking Down Silos Still Works." *Harvard Business Review.* September 09, 2015,

Boeing Knowledge Management, 2015. NASA 2020, Tim Bridges, Director of Knowledge Management Engineering, Operations and Technology.

Festinger, L. (Ed.). 1964. *Conflict, decision, and dissonance (Vol. 3).* Stanford, CA. Stanford University Press.

Garvin, David A. 1993. "Building a Learning Organization." *Harvard Business Review* July-August 1993.

Macondo Investigation Report Volume 3 4/17/2016, Chemical Safety Board.

Senge, Peter M. 1990. *The Fifth Discipline: The Art & Practice of the Learning Organization.* New York: Doubleday.

Six Amazing Years, RAGs, NATOPS and More, Vice Admiral Robert F. Dunn, U.S. Navy

Conclusion

Throughout this book I have shared lessons from tragic airline accidents that evolved aviation safety, but these lessons came at a cost – a cost of seven aircraft and 824 lives. After reviewing these tragic cockpit voice recorders transcripts, we all agree that none of these accidents should have happened. But they did. And they highlighted that the airline industry relied too much on pilot/human judgment to get the job done right. Black boxes were key to understanding why pilots/humans made basic, fundamental human errors while at work – errors that were bucketed in the past as not following procedures or incompetency. But the airlines were driven to not stop at the "fifth why." Instead, corporate leadership learned that their tragic accidents, previously labelled as "pilot error", were actually failures of System 1 and System 2 – an overdue acknowledgment.

With an acceptance that the human will err, the industry was able to learn why we err. It uncovered cognitive biases, the power of worker relationships, prospective memory, channelized attention and the list goes on.

The airline industry moved away from generating safety alerts to change frontline behavior to tools that were designed to prevent the reoccurrence of another accident. Strategically, these tools have been housed within standardization departments. Standardization departments that exist to instill systematic learnings that changes the behavior of an entire corporation – not just an individual. Standardization that delivers human quality and delivers the right stuff.

Index

About the Author

Andrew Dingee is a graduate of the University of Illinois. He is a 27-year veteran of the U.S. Marines where he flew AV8Bs. During his tours, he received over one dozen awards for outstanding airmanship and safety.

In 1999, he was hired at a major U.S. airline where he held a variety of safety leadership positions and flew B727s, B737s and A320s. For his commercial aviation safety accomplishments, he was nominated for the Flight Safety Foundation Brownlow award. Andrew has authored numerous white papers on human factors and standardization. Since 2010, Andrew has been an international advocate for using lessons from commercial aviation safety to revolutionize other industries. Andrew and his wife, Valerie, make their home in Houston, Texas.